THE MOVIE PRODUCER

THE
MOVIE
PRODUCER

———

A Handbook for Producing and Picture-Making

———

Paul N. Lazarus III

BARNES & NOBLE BOOKS
A DIVISION OF HARPER & ROW, PUBLISHERS
New York, Cambridge, Philadelphia, San Francisco,
London, Mexico City, São Paulo, Singapore, Sydney

FIRST EDITION

Designer: C. Linda Dingler

Library of Congress Cataloging in Publication Data

Lazarus, Paul N.
  The movie producer.

  Includes index.
  1. Moving-pictures—Production and direction.   I. Title.
PN1995.9.P7L36   1985   791.43'0232   84-43185
ISBN 0-06-463724-7 (pbk.)

85 86 87 88 89 MPC 10 9 8 7 6 5 4 3 2 1

Contents

Preface

This book grows out of a course I gave at UCLA on the role of the producer in today's motion picture industry. In familiarizing myself with the literature, I discovered that there were no books that purported to explain how the process of getting movies made really works. For a business that requires no degrees or licenses to enter, it seemed a surprising void. There are plenty of biographies to read, but no works that look at the nuts and bolts of producing. This book, then, is an attempt to meet that need.

I come to this effort from the vantage point of having been a lawyer, agent, film executive, and film producer. I have produced six theatrical motion pictures (*ECU*, *Westworld*, *Futureworld*, *Capricorn One*, *Hanover Street*, and *Barbarosa*) and have been head of production for three mini-majors, as the new financing entities are familiarly called.

In these various capacities, I have had an opportunity to watch the filmmaking process from different perspectives and different sides of the desk. Still, it is not easy to arrive at a workable definition of a producer. My now-grown children have often asked me what a producer does. They have become weary, by this time, with my inability to come up with an acceptable answer. In part, this book is the belated response to their question.

Credits that appear on films and in newspaper advertising rarely furnish helpful information in defining what a producer does. The titles—executive producer, co-producer, or producer—speak more to the structure of the business deal than they do to job functions or descriptions.

It is even more troublesome to examine the job done by a single producer in an effort to understand what producers do. There are producers who physically produce pictures on location, producers who make deals, who raise money, who stay close to "bankable" stars, and who perform a host of other functions. Each, in his way, is performing some facet of a producer's overall responsibility of getting a picture developed, mounted, and sold. To reach some understanding about what a producer is and does, then, it is easier to look at the filmmaking process as a whole and identify the producer's role throughout. By taking this broader view, a more clearly defined picture of the producer will emerge.

I have divided the producer's role, in this sense, into three basic areas—development, production, and marketing. To an extent, these headings are arbitrary and serve only the convenience of the author. As such, they allow for the inclusion of those areas of effort that I have come to feel are essential for a producer who understands his craft. His choices after that are his own. Critical and commercial success have been carved out by many producers who chose unique and untried routes. Underlying most of their successes is a keen sense of entrepreneurism. This may come to the fore at any stage of picture-making—from obtaining the rights to a project to marketing a film with flair and showmanship.

This book is written for the reader seeking information on producing and on the processes at work in today's motion picture industry. It assumes the reader will not be endowed, at this stage, with the muscle or clout required to pick up the phone and talk to either Robert Redford or the president of Columbia Pictures. Someone who can pull off either of these feats will have different strategies to employ than those offered in this book. *The Movie Producer*, finally, is for those who either want to take positive steps toward achieving this status or who simply want to know more of what it is all about.

I owe much to many in connection with the writing of this book. I am especially indebted to my friends who patiently allowed their business days to be interrupted by my questions, and who continued their involvement by offering invaluable suggestions through the editing process. David Comsky, Michael Crichton, Mark Damon, Alan Freeman, Anthony Goldschmidt, Leo Greenfield, Philip Hacker, Peter Hyams, James Potter, Michael Rachmil, Bill Robinson, and Arlene Sellers are all people with whom I have worked over the years. I count them as friends and as colleagues and am most grateful for their help. Particular thanks is owed to Laurie Pozmantier, whose unflagging enthusiasm and editorial assistance contributed a great deal to the final shape of this book.

Malibu, California

I

DEVELOPMENT

1

Acquisition of Rights

The genesis of motion pictures can be traced to many different sources. Before they existed in screenplay form, they may have begun as original ideas, treatments, short stories, books, plays, songs, magazine articles, or even news stories. The motion picture rights to the underlying or source material must be obtained before it can be adapted into a movie.

A DEFINITION OF "RIGHTS"

In simple terms, a right is permission by the owner of a property to utilize his work. This permission may entail the right to use it in the medium for which it was created, such as performing a play on stage, or the right to adapt it to another medium, such as turning a book into a movie. The owner or creator of property of this kind is protected from unauthorized use by both the Copyright Act, a federal law, and by long-established legal precedents.

Perhaps the single most important thing that an aspiring producer can do is to obtain motion picture rights to a property. For the producer seeking to put a project together, obtaining rights to a property is the first step toward credibility and toward successfully mounting a production. But to compete in this arena, the new producer should acquire a working knowledge of the basic components involved in the acquisition of rights. Rights are obtained by purchase or by an option agreement which provides the exclusive opportunity to subsequently purchase them. The aspiring producer must also realize that the pursuit of material is highly competitive. In addition to television networks and motion picture studios, the marketplace is filled with independent producers, all of whom regard rights to material as the very lifeblood of the picture-making process.

MOTION PICTURE MATERIAL

As with so many other facets of the motion picture industry, at the heart of the acquisition process is the ability to write your own check. The price tag on a given piece of material may put it out of reach of all but the most well-financed buyers. While there are a few exceptions, generally hit Broadway shows and best-selling books are simply out of reach for the independent producer.

The first tenet in the acquisition of rights process, then, is to reach for what you can afford. If you require the backing of a studio or other financier to acquire material for you, as most producers do, then your choices in material will be more limited than those producers who have the ability to self-finance. A basic truth of the motion picture business is that most material is represented by literary or motion picture agents, and they are far more disposed to submit material to potential buyers than to potential middlemen.

As one studies the market, certain patterns begin to emerge. In the case of important best-sellers, the beginning producer should be aware of the very long odds against his involvement. In the first place, he is unlikely to be able to do anything more than take such a best-seller to a studio and ask it to purchase the book for him. In the sophisticated publishing world of today, such books are probably well represented by experienced literary agents. Over the years, these agents have developed close relationships with certain studios, producers, and directors. The great likelihood is that any book represented by them will be submitted first to their closest contacts.

Even before literary agents see manuscripts or galleys of a book, editors at publishing houses are exposed to the material. It is an open secret that many of these editors have financial arrangements with members of the motion picture community and provide their motion picture contacts with a first look at promising material. Even if one is sufficiently close to an editor or an agent to be able to see material at this early stage, it is rare to have an exclusive hold on it without actually optioning it or purchasing it. Frequently a studio executive receives the same new book (often copied from the same Xerox machine) from more than one producer. In that case, the producers have not put up their own money but are instead seeking financing from the studio. Some studios in that situation will endeavor to protect the first submitter. Others recognize no responsibility, moral or legal, to a producer who submits a book that he does not own.

Sources of material that have grown considerably in recent years are the breaking news story and investigative journalism. Producers have found that these areas provide a rich lode of material for motion pictures. A project such as *Urban Cowboy,* for example, began in the world of magazine publishing. Likewise, the film *Silkwood* depicted the events of an actual person's life that received wide newspaper coverage. Many contend that the major newspapers in the country are the richest source for motion picture material. This area has become hotly competitive primarily because of the continuing interest shown by the television networks in adapting real-life dramas into movies for television. Since the amounts of money that may be required to option a real-life drama are considerably less than would be required for a best-selling book, this is a fruitful area for the aspiring producer to examine. It is also an area where diligence and enthusiasm will often prevail over experience. There are numerous instances where the rights in a breaking story were optioned to an inexperienced producer who was willing to get on a plane and go to the scene rather than making contact by telephone.

ACQUIRING THE RIGHTS

Obvious commercial subjects will most likely be the object of heated competitive bidding. Still, there is always reason to inquire into the availability of motion picture rights because you have nothing to lose and considerable information to gain. To determine if motion picture rights are available for a book, look for the name of the publisher on the title page and place a call to the subsidiary rights department of that publishing house. The publisher may refer you to the author's representative, usually a lawyer or an agent. In a few cases, the motion picture rights are held by the publisher, allowing the producer to deal directly with the publishing company.

If it is determined that the rights are available, the producer should take a hard look at the situation before investing his money. Most novels are offered for motion picture production at the time of their publication. Very few are actually optioned or purchased. They are reviewed by studio literary departments, usually rejected, and the reports on them filed away. A property that has already been turned down by a studio has one strike against it. A negative report or reader's coverage exists somewhere in the studio files and will certainly be exhumed in the event of a resubmission. If the book is to overcome this handicap, the producer must come up with a unique approach or secure an attractive element, such as a writer, a director, or a star, who will carry sufficient weight to overcome the already negative studio reaction. However difficult, this has been accomplished countless times in the past.

It should not be forgotten that while there may be negative coverage on file, it is likely that the book was never read by the studio executives then in power, only by a studio reader. So much material is received by a studio each week, usually on the order of seventy-five to 100 submissions, that no executive could possibly read everything. Readers fill this breach by examining submissions and writing synopses with their recommendations. If the reader doesn't respond positively to the material, it is customarily rejected without further discussion. The studio production executive may have only a dim awareness of the material at this point. Moreover, the average tenure of a studio head is a mere two years. Thus, material submitted in prior administrations may be completely unfamiliar to him. For this reason, a unique point of view and an enthusiastic approach can well offset a reader's negative report.

There are untold numbers of properties that are not protected by copyright and exist in what is known as the public domain. Such properties are available without the need for rights payments and may provide a fertile area for the aspiring producer in his quest for motion picture subjects. Works by Shakespeare or Charles Dickens, for example, exist in the public domain and may be used as motion picture properties without having to acquire any rights.

Such material antedated the Copyright Act. Other material may not have been published in accordance with all the formalities required by that legislation, or in some other way may have fallen into the public domain. While such material may now be used without the necessity of negotiating rights from a holder of a copyright, there are other concerns that the producer must keep in mind. If the material is based on the life of a real person, there may be laws in some states affording protection to the subject of the piece. Since such doctrines vary from state to state and since case law is very much in flux, the producer is well advised to consult qualified counsel if he finds himself dealing in this area.

Most published material, however, is copyrighted. It is generally possible to do a copyright search to ascertain where the motion picture rights currently stand. The Washington, D.C., law firm of Brylawski & Cleary specializes in copyright searches. Such searches reveal the complete chain of title of the property in question. Any option, assignment, or other rights transaction involving that material would surface in this kind of search. These searches cost a comparatively small amount of money and are essential if the producer is serious about optioning or purchasing movie rights.

If the producer simply does not have enough money on hand to complete a reasonable deal with an author, it may benefit the producer to try another approach. He might make a personal appeal to the author in hopes of structuring a deal on some kind of joint venture basis. While most authors have surrounded themselves with sophisticated advisers, there is little to lose by making a stab at some form of co-production arrangement. Typically, this arrangement would provide the author with a small or even a token option payment but would enable him to retain a very substantial equity in the project. In effect, the author is made a partner of the producer rather than merely paid a sum of money for his work. If the material is not the object of competitive bidding, such an approach could conceivably prove attractive to an author.

Finally, the aspiring producer should not overlook his friends or acquaintances who have written screenplays. By joining forces with a friend on a handshake deal, a project may develop some momentum which could culminate in a picture getting financed. Down the road, if the project does move toward becoming a reality, the handshake deal should be put into a more formal arrangement for the protection of both parties. Contacts with writers are an invaluable assist to the producer seeking viable material.

NEGOTIATING THE OPTION

Once the producer has identified the property he is seeking and ascertained the rights status, in most cases he will try to negotiate an option for the rights. In the motion picture business, options are in common use. An option is the right to acquire something by the subsequent payment of additional money. Thus, by paying a comparatively small sum, the producer acquires the "right" to buy "rights" he seeks within a prescribed time period. While option payments are of course subject to negotiation, as a general rule they approximate 10 percent of the total purchase price. For example, if the motion picture rights to a given book were pegged at $100,000, it might be possible to option those same rights for $10,000 for a specified time period. During that time, the producer could try to put his movie together by arranging his financing, having a screenplay written, or assembling the elements to do the film. In the event he chose to exercise his option within his prescribed term, he would have to pay an additional $90,000 to acquire the rights.

RENEWAL PERIOD

It should be noted that it is *frequently* the case that a one-year period, a typical option term, is not enough time to get a project off the ground. For that reason, most producers will also negotiate a renewal period of an additional six months or one year. This will require a further payment to the author which may or may not be applicable against the overall purchase price. It is not unusual for the author to demand, as a condition for extending the option period, some progress toward getting the movie made. As an example, the producer may have to secure one or more of the important elements: the services of a director, a star, or a screenwriter before the option period can be extended. In this way, the author has some control over whether his property is on its way to being made into a film or has been simply put on the shelf.

Under ordinary circumstances, an option agreement would be negotiated at the same time as a purchase agreement. This is only logical since no one would be in favor of going back to the bargaining table at the time an option is exercised and the rights are acquired. Over the years, the form of both of these agreements has become reasonably standardized, although the ingenuity of lawyers and agents does keep them evolving into more and more complex formats. Still, certain basic provisions are common to all such agreements.

The option agreement specifies what rights are being optioned, the mechanics of exercising or extending an option, the term of the option period, and the compensation or consideration for the author. The author or owner of the material would, in turn, make certain representations and warranties as to the originality and ownership of the work. It is of course vital that the producer have such safeguards built into the framework of the deal.

PURCHASE AGREEMENTS

In order to understand the scope of a purchase agreement, it is easiest to envision the rights involved in any material as a bundle, much like a cable with many different strands of wire running through it. Each strand represents a different right, some of which may be acquired by the producer, and some of which may be retained or reserved by the author. Motion picture rights are but one strand among many. Publication rights, radio rights, dramatic rights, merchandising rights, and a host of others are all on the table when a negotiation is commenced. When the producer negotiates with the seller or owner of a property, he will generally try to secure as many rights for as little money as possible. Conversely, the seller will try to restrict the grant of rights as narrowly as he can, reserving to himself all the rights not specifically granted. It follows that he will endeavor to secure as much money for the rights granted as he possibly can. Negotiations of this kind are sufficiently sophisticated that different payments will be settled upon for the different rights that may be granted. Motion picture rights will thus typically cost more than the rights to adapt material into a two-hour movie for television. This is consistent with the fact that the budgets for movies for television average far less than the budgets of theatrical films.

THE LAWYER'S INVOLVEMENT

It becomes quickly apparent that option and purchase agreements are anything but casual documents. Accordingly, the producer is ill-advised to negotiate these agreements without the help of an attorney. A lawyer very experienced in this field is David Comsky, Esq., of the Beverly Hills law firm of Freshman, Mulvaney, Marantz, Comsky, Cahan & Deutsch. Comsky makes the point that "Lawyers' fees will increase a producer's costs at the beginning, but will save money and heartache in the long run." When a financing source someday forces the producer to go back to renegotiate with the seller because the job wasn't done correctly the first time around, it can only result in extended problems and expense for the producer. Better to use an attorney the first time through, and better yet to use one skilled in this field. "Whether it is the entertainment industry or real estate, it is preferable to stay with people who are experienced in the specific areas involved. They tend to know the parameters on both sides and don't take indefensible or outrageous positions which endlessly protract the negotiations," adds Comsky.

In point of fact, the experienced lawyer should be able to prepare an agreement utilizing a familiar format which requires less negotiation than one might assume. Often the major points of disagreement concern dollars and time periods. This is more a matter for business negotiation than it is for legal negotiation. A qualified entertainment attorney will be able to offer business guidelines to the producer which can be very helpful in conducting a negotiation.

AUTHORS' COMPENSATION

Many authors today, through their representatives, will seek some form of deferred compensation as part of their rights payment. This is common practice, since there is much equity in the position: If something wonderful happens with the author's work, he is entitled to additional sums of money. In many instances this thinking leads to the negotiation of escalators in the purchase price based on the performance of the book in hardbound or paperback sales. Thus, if the book sells a certain number of copies, or if the book appears for a certain number of weeks on a designated best-seller list, the author will be entitled to additional compensation. Further payments may also be due the author if he has negotiated a percentage of profits from any film made from his work.

The amount of compensation to the owner or author of the material involved in these negotiations is subject to wide swings, depending on the amount of interest the material has generated. It is again helpful to be assisted in these negotiations by an experienced entertainment law practitioner. There are financial parameters to any rights deal, as well as certain minimal provisions that most studios or other financing entities will insist upon. Guidance during the early negotiations with an author or his representative will prove of inestimable importance should the project proceed into production.

Even with the utmost care and precision in the negotiation and drafting stages of a rights acquisition, it is very common for a successful movie to spawn a host of lawsuits by litigants claiming that their works have been plagiarized. Two profitable films that I produced, *Westworld* and *Capricorn One,* brought forth half a dozen claims of copyright infringement. In both instances, the screenplays were original to the writer-directors involved, and all claims were successfully defended by the insurance carrier working for the picture. Virtually all films carry an insurance policy known as an errors and omissions policy, which protects the film and its backers from claims of those asserting copyright infringement. Most such cases are successfully defended without ever coming to trial. This is almost certainly the result of the fact that most feature films are *not* based upon plagiarized material. Representations and warranties, together with an arduous review process all along the way, tend to smoke out questionable material before it progresses to being a feature film.

In the main, the movie business is not characterized by frequent thievery of ideas or material. This is a common fear of most inexperienced producers and it usually turns out to be groundless. The overwhelming majority of professionals, either in studios or operating as independents, would not contemplate ripping off material. In any event, copyrighting material or availing oneself of the registration procedures of the Writer's Guild affords very good protection. The latter technique permits the registration of material by a member or nonmember of the Guild for the nominal payment of $10. This will establish the date that material was within one's control and may prove critically important in the event of a subsequent claim. Similarly, the procedure of mailing material to oneself by registered mail will establish a date at which material was controlled. Lastly, a copyright can be secured by completing the required forms and paying the prescribed fee.

The most common error in rights acquisitions is as mundane as forgetting to exercise an option before it runs out. As silly as this sounds, this error is made over and over by the most experienced producers and even by studios. Of course, if an option expires without being renewed or exercised, all hold on the material will be lost. Most authors' representatives relish this situation, since it permits them to resell the rights at terms at least as favorable as those that existed under their prior arrangement. This problem can be easily avoided by maintaining a calendar file which alerts you to the impending option date. While this is simplicity itself, the mistake of letting an option expire is made over and over in the course of everyday business.

One of the greatest advantages in optioning or purchasing a piece of material on one's own is the opportunity it affords to control the creative direction of the project. It allows the producer flexibility and time to assemble elements of a motion picture package and to discuss further development costs without the pressure of being under the gun. Being one of several producers running with the same material or dashing about to different financiers with a 48-hour start on the rest of the producing community may work out for the best, but it certainly has its limitations. There is a much greater likelihood that expedience or creative compromise will not play as great a role in the process when the producer has a definite term during which he controls the rights to his material. He will be able to submit the material to writers and directors and discuss with them their reactions and their visions before simply surrendering the material to the process of trying to get a movie made. This is an important step, since films are ultimately a collaboration among several creative elements. The producer who seeks to package his film with a writer or a director ideally will have time to explore the respective points of view on material with potential collaborators before rushing into a decision. This is the best insurance that everyone has the same kind of movie in mind before actually setting out to make it.

As indicated earlier, the most pervasive constraint on the producer's ability to work with care and deliberation during the development process is his ability to self-finance the steps along the way, from acquisition of the rights on. Once other hands are on the oars, other voices will inevitably be heard. Again, this need not be destructive to the development of the project and may indeed produce salutary results. It is certainly something that must be watched closely however, throughout the development and the making of the picture.

A producer who secures an option on a piece of material earns an initial measure of respect from the studios. In an era where the word "producer" has come to mean many different things, an option at least demonstrates the producer's motivation, follow-through, and belief in the project. While not an overwhelming factor in a negotiation with a financing source, the acquisition of an option on one's own does provide something of an edge in business dealings with studios.

Producers seem drawn to material because it strikes some

responsive chord in them, or because they think it is salable, or for both reasons. Sometimes, as with *Chariots of Fire, Rocky,* or even *Star Wars,* the vision of the producer-filmmaker triumphs in spite of the fear or concern of the financing entity. The determination of the producer in a situation like this will be severely tested.

Two points do stand out with some clarity: The producer's vision of the project is often the thin strand on which the whole movie will be hung, and that vision usually begins with a piece of material. Many things can go wrong before that vision is transformed into a film and placed before the public. Without a conviction of that kind, movies such as *Yentl, One Flew Over the Cuckoo's Nest, Chariots of Fire, Rocky,* or *Gandhi* would never have gotten made. The essential first step is to find material that you believe in, acquire a hold on the rights, and set about the process of developing the material into a movie.

2

Agents

Some years ago, as an inexperienced agent, I was witness to a series of telephone calls made by the head of the motion picture department of a major agency to prospective purchasers of a screenplay. Each buyer, studio executive or producer, was given a variation of the same speech. Each was told that he had an exclusive hold on the material, two days before his competitors would see it. When the calls were completed, I asked the agent how he could lie to each person he spoke with and keep a clear conscience. Without missing a beat, he replied that "There is a special place in Heaven for agents." They occupy a special place on earth as well.

The talent agent wields much power in the motion picture industry today. The agent plays a pivotal role for the new producer because in the motion picture industry few pictures are put together without the services of an agent somewhere along the way. The talent agent is privy to specialized information about what is happening, where it is happening, and who is making it happen, and he also has the entree and influence to materially affect the process.

The heads of the motion picture departments of the major talent agencies—International Creative Management, the William Morris Agency, and Creative Artists Agency—through their relationships with the top echelon of studio executives and independent producers, are the most potent force in Hollywood in getting pictures made. Forget the media-encouraged view that all agents are named Bernie and are short, cigar-smoking hustlers. They are as varied as people can be, and they possess a variety of different skills.

THE AGENCY

As a business, agencies are not difficult to understand. With the exception of a relative handful of unscrupulous operators, agencies are legitimate businesses that commission a state-authorized maximum of 10 percent of their client's gross income in compensation for work done on his behalf. Thus, if a client received a $50,000 fee for a film, the agent would be entitled to $5,000 for the services he performed. If the client further received additional monies as deferred compensation or from a percentage of the film's profits, the agent would be entitled to 10 percent of these sums as well. It should be noted that agency commissions are payable to the agency as a whole, not to the individual agent who makes the deal. He is a salaried corporate employee.

Agencies are licensed by the state and franchised by the various professional guilds such as the Screen Actors Guild (SAG), the Directors Guild of America (DGA), and the American Federation of Television and Radio Artists (AFTRA). These franchise agreements between the agencies and the guilds provide maximum terms for client representation as well as those circumstances that would allow a guild member to leave an agency. Failure of the agent to find offers of employment for the guild member, or the departure of a designated agent(s) from the agency, may create a right on the part of the client to leave the agency.

Agents are middlemen, operating between sellers and buyers. They are not necessary to the making of a deal, but their influence is almost always a factor. In the agency firmament, there are large and small agencies. In Los Angeles alone, there are nearly 300 agencies of which nine would be classified as middle-size, and only three—ICM, William Morris, and CAA—as large. Some agencies restrict their representation to writers and directors, and others only to performers. Some specialize in representing clients active in the television industry; others specialize in the motion picture industry. The largest agencies have offices at different locations both in America and abroad. With as many as 200 agents or other support people in their employ, these agencies have sufficient manpower to amass all the pertinent information available on an international basis. This is less a tribute to their brilliant information-gathering network, or even to their basic competence, and more to the effectiveness of an army in the field covering the needs of buyers all over the world.

Within a large agency, information regarding activities of buyers or needs of clients is exchanged several times a week at staff meetings. Although a client may have one or two principal agents working on his behalf, all the resources of a large agency are there to be galvanized into action to get a specific part or find a buyer for a particular project.

The smaller agency offers something else to its clients. Bill Robinson of the Beverly Hills talent agency of Robinson and Luttrell has been a fixture in the small agency world for twenty years. He represents a handful of established actors as well as several writers. Robinson's perspective is that, compared to the larger agencies, the close personal attention he is able to pay each of his clients more than compensates for what he gives up in the way of information. Speaking of his client Carol Burnett, Robinson says, "She is more concerned with the *kind* of representation she receives than in having a large agency with many high-powered dealmakers behind her. Her priority is on a relationship based on trust where she can speak openly and honestly about her career choices." That may or may not be possible in a large agency, where the needs of scores of clients must be given attention.

The small agency must be prepared to retain the services of specialists should one of its clients move into an unfamiliar area. For example, if Carol Burnett wishes to write a book and therefore needs guidance in choosing a publisher and setting the terms of a deal, Robinson would retain a top publishing attorney and work with him in making the deal. In a large agency, on the other hand, the client would be referred to the agency's own book specialists, and in concert with the client's regular agent for movies and television, a deal would be recommended. It is not possible to say that one method is better than the other. The particular needs of the client should govern the choice of a large or a small agency.

The super agent, particularly at one of the three big companies, has a wealth of information at his fingertips. He has numerous junior agents telephoning and visiting all the studios and the independent buyers, ascertaining the needs, present and future, of all the players in the motion picture game. The agent can then strategize how best to put his clients to work.

To know who represents whom among the various agencies, a producer should avail himself of a little-heralded but extremely useful service offered by the Screen Actors Guild. On request, it will furnish the name and telephone numbers of the agents of its members. This can be of great assistance to the producer trying to put a project together, since it provides up-to-the-minute information about an actor's representatives.

SECURING AN AGENT

It is important for the producer to know how to plug into the strength and muscle of a powerful agent. This is not an easy task. It means convincing an agent that there is something to gain from involvement with you. Nonetheless it can be done. Agents, like any salesmen, prefer to sell what is easiest to sell. Agents would much rather have the telephone ring all day with offers for their hot clients than have to undertake the more arduous tasks of building a career or selling a client who has no heat attached to him. Heat is that peculiar phenomenon that describes a sudden demand for a client (or a script, or any other commodity in the marketplace). Heat most often goes hand in hand with commercial success, although the success may be solely in the eyes of the beholder. It is very possible for a star to be red hot because Hollywood perceives his as yet unreleased film to be a huge hit. Should the film not open well, the heat surrounding its star can disappear overnight.

I experienced a dilemma like this when I was slated to produce the Willie Nelson film *Barbarosa* which was to follow his film *Honeysuckle Rose*. The industry experts branded *Honeysuckle Rose* a hit before its release and Willie Nelson, accordingly, became a very hot commodity. When the film opened to disappointing business, not only was the bloom off the rose, but, for the moment, off Willie Nelson as well.

It is a fact of agency life that not all clients can be hot at any one time. Most clients require some degree of salesmanship to get work, and most agents avidly pursue their client's next job. For this reason, the door to an agency is always open to the producer who has something to offer its clients. However, in most cases, the new producer will be unable to deliver what most agents prefer, a firm offer of employment. Instead, the aspiring producer may have only the beginnings of a project to put on the table. *It is enough.* The producer's conviction about a good or unique idea is more than enough to open serious conversations with an agent. It is very much in the agent's, and thus his client's, best interest to explore where all such conversations might lead.

While it is nice to hope that the agent who responds to your inquiry will become wildly excited and will be a superstar agent in his own right, the reality is often somewhat different. Absent the involvement of a big-name star or director early on, the strongest likelihood is that the producer will find a greater receptivity from the ranks of the junior or middle range of agents. This is the group most likely to have clients who stand to benefit from an early involvement with a project and a producer. The critical point is that the interest and hopefully the passion of *some* agent can be secured and will prove of vital assistance to the producer attempting to get his project off the ground.

Sometimes just speaking with an agent may prove a difficult undertaking. If your name is unknown to the agent, you may find that your calls go unanswered. This is not something to be taken personally. It is an all too commonplace occurrence. Here are a couple of suggestions for remedying this predicament.

If you are able to have a friend of the agent's make a call on your behalf, do so. It will usually get you a telephone response, if not a meeting, and then you are on your own. If this alternative is not open to you, you might befriend the secretary who answers the agent's phone. This is less manipulative than it sounds. Many agents consider their secretaries to be agents in training and regularly have them handle many of the functions of agentry, from administrative work to reading scripts. Therefore, instead of regarding the secretary, male or female, as minor clerical help, you would be well advised to introduce yourself, ask for his or her name, and strike up some kind of conversation. It is very common for secretaries to read submitted material, and, if they like it, to recommend it to the agents they work for, or even to another agent within the agency. Persistence and resourcefulness not only help in this pursuit, they are probably a necessity. Agents are busy people who work under considerable pressure. Your call, as an unknown producer, is the easiest call for them to duck.

For the producer hoping to secure a commitment from an actor for his project, there are pitfalls in going directly to the actor and bypassing the agent. Some agents get very squirrelly when they feel that a producer has gone behind their backs. Other agents are not bothered by such behavior and tend to focus only on the merits of the project and the deal. Often there is no way to know where a particular agent stands on this sensitive question before wading into it. If you guess wrong, you may find yourself dealing with a hostile agent who can make it all but impossible for you to obtain the services of his client. As a general rule, the agent should be sounded out in the first instance and his assistance sought. If these overtures prove fruitless, try to make direct contact with the actor. But unless you have a personal relationship with the actor, he will usually refer the matter back to his agent.

Agencies are not monolithic creations. They are collections of individuals and the best tack a producer can take is to establish working relationships with at least one agent in as many agencies as he can. In this way he can tap into the informational resources of the agencies as well as enlist the services of agents who may genuinely spark to his project. Significantly, the producer doesn't necessarily need an agent's help for his own representation as much as he needs it to gain access to elements for his project and to buyers. Very few producers have signed exclusive representation agreements with agents in the motion picture area. Where the agent has proven useful on a project by effecting an introduction or otherwise helping to package the material, it is not uncommon for the producer to let the agent represent him on that project and pay the required 10 percent commission on monies he receives. Many feel this is an added motivation to the agent to work hard to try to put a deal together.

Depending upon the producer's circumstances, dealing with large agencies may be alternately rewarding and frustrating. If he must attract a major star to his project, he will discover that well over 90 percent of the actors or actresses recognized as stars are represented by a mere dozen agencies. Naturally, the largest agencies represent the overwhelming majority. Access to such performers is best facilitated by the producer's establishing and maintaining good working relationships throughout the agency world.

The agent's responsibilities have been described in terms of three S's: Signing, Selling, and Servicing. Most agents have the ability to sign clients. They have to put themselves on the line and risk personal rejection. Without exception, however, successful agents have all mastered the art of inspiring confidence in themselves and persuading others to sign with them as clients.

Selling is an obvious component of a successful agent's makeup. Whether the agent is involved in selling a star or an unknown, it is still the agent's single most important responsibility. There will be different problems in finding work for an unknown versus a major star, but both tasks are at the core of successful agentry. Jobs have to be uncovered, buyers convinced, clients assured, and proper deals negotiated. This is what being an agent is all about.

The last part of an agent's responsibility involves servicing, which is the establishment and maintenance of a relationship with the client based on confidence and trust. As Bill Robinson puts it, "The client must have the feeling that you truly care and that you are doing the best job you possibly can." From the client's viewpoint, this is often as important as getting the job itself. It is only in this kind of atmosphere that the inevitable difficult decisions can be properly faced. This career guidance portion of the agent's responsibility is greatly facilitated by a close working relationship rooted in mutual trust and respect. This is the agent–client relationship at its best.

Of the three functions of signing, selling, and servicing, some agents will excel more at one than the others. Some agents are great salesmen, others are great "closers," getting new clients to sign with an agency, while still others have tremendous innate abilities in knowing what is right for a client at any particular moment. The most successful and most powerful agents combine skills in all these areas. The producer should not be surprised to discover, however, that such skills are not common to all agents at every agency.

PACKAGING

A word much bandied about in today's marketplace is "packaging." It is a critical component of the super agents' work at the large agencies and the dream of most smaller agents who ply their trade in the motion picture industry. Packaging means the combining of two or more elements, such as a writer, actor, or director, into a single project which is then presented to prospective financiers. Generally, the packaging agent will commission 10 percent of the gross compensation of each of his clients involved in the package. It is not unheard of, however, for the buyer to also compensate the agent with a packaging fee for steering the package in his direction.

From the buyer's standpoint, a package serves to remove much of the risk inherent in development. By offering a buyer a script, an actor, and a director, the buyer can make an intelligent decision on both the creative and financial aspects of a project. A package removes much of the buyer's anxiety about spending large sums for a script and then not being able to secure a director or actor for the project. That work has been done for him by the agent-packager.

In the past, motion picture studios were more active in the packaging game because they had so many people under exclusive contract. It was very simple to package a film because it only entailed notifying individuals under contract that they were to report to a certain sound stage at a designated time. It is considerably more difficult to put a picture together in today's world where few people are under exclusive contract and everyone is pursuing the same actors and directors.

From the agent's standpoint, there are several advantages to a package. The obvious one is that it can provide a vehicle for two or more clients to work in. Using the argument that the whole is worth more than the sum of its parts, the agent may also be able to raise the prices of his clients if they are combined into a package. Lastly, a package may be strong enough for the agent to demand that the financier not consider the submission for a development deal, but rather commit to make the film and thus guarantee all of the fees involved. This forces the financier to abandon his customary go-slow manner and substitutes a picture commitment for the more usual development deal. A development deal, as the term suggests, is an arrangement to further develop a project in the hope that it will someday be made into a motion picture. Guaranteed fees mean guaranteed commissions and that means a happy agent and happy clients.

It is possible that the agent will not have the right element within his stable of clients to complete a package. He can then use his inside knowledge to attempt to attract someone else's client to the package. A reputation as a packager is a wonderful tool in signing new clients as it presents the packaging agent in a very good light. Many is the actor who feels, and often with considerable justification, that his career would be greatly enhanced if he had the packaging capabilities of a major agent behind him.

Packaging, however, is not without risks. Performers, and often directors and screenwriters, have notoriously fragile personalities. They can easily become convinced that their careers are being "handled" rather than guided and that they are being forced into projects for the agent's convenience rather than for the benefits to their careers.

A recent film provides an interesting case study of such a problem. The film *All Night Long* was set up at Universal Pictures by super agent Sue Mengers with her husband, Jean-Claude Tremont, directing and her client Gene Hackman starring opposite Lisa Eichhorn. For whatever the reason, Eichhorn didn't work out, and when the smoke cleared she had been replaced by Mengers' premier client, Barbra Streisand. The project turned into a situation with a commercially problematic script, a director married to the packager and undertaking his first major film, and a huge star stepping into a smaller role than she was accustomed to playing. Of course, Streisand had the final say on whether she wanted to do this project. It would not be unusual for the agent to have had considerable influence in the decision, however. In any event, by the time the final curtain was rung down on *All Night Long,* Miss Streisand was no longer represented by Miss Mengers.

If the severance between Miss Streisand and Miss Mengers was actually caused or influenced by the latter's becoming involved in the package, the foregoing story will illustrate the inherent risks of packaging, particularly when it involves an agent's important clients. Judged by the time and energy that major agents devote to packaging, however, it can be concluded that they believe that the benefits far outweigh the risks.

THE "FIRM OFFERS ONLY" DILEMMA

Another area of concern for agents, and thus for producers hoping to enlist the help of an agent, is whether their client can be approached without the benefit of a firm offer. Many agents are unwilling to put such projects in front of their clients for fear that if the client likes it the agent may not be able to secure the assignment.

It is an understandable dilemma from the agent's point of view. Most agents, particularly at the large agencies, have to deal with so many clients that they can't establish close and trusting relationships with all of them. For that reason, many agents are reluctant to start the ball rolling on a project that may never materialize, or worse still, will come into being without the services of their client.

For the producer, one answer to this problem is surprisingly simple. That is, tell the whole truth and nothing but the truth. Of course, there will always be some agents who will not act without a firm offer. But a great number of reluctant agents can be swayed if they are filled in on all the details. The reason for this is that they can in turn put the real facts in front of their client. It is not difficult for an agent to say, for example, that he has been given very interesting material but that the director is not sure about the actor in question, or that the film has not yet been given a firm "go," but that it appears imminent. Then, the onus shifts to the client. If he says he understands and will read it anyway, the agent is effectively off the hook. If the client reads it and likes it, he will then know that the best the agent can do is work hard in his behalf to secure the part. It is helpful in this process if the agent can report to his client that he has read and liked the script and met and liked the producer. By giving the agent the straight story and not trying to out-maneuver him, the producer will have done what he can to bring his project to the desired actor's attention.

It should be noted that because there are fewer films being made today, the "firm offers only" policy is less in evidence and more and more agents are playing an increasingly helpful role in trying to get pictures made. The new producer should be aware of this turn and enlist such help wherever he can find it.

If you are in hot pursuit of one of the handful of so-called bankable stars, the likelihood is that you will be competing with many projects with firm offers attached. A bankable star is one whom a picture can be financed around—someone whom bankers would unhesitatingly finance in a feature film. Such stars as Robert Redford, Meryl Streep, Dustin Hoffman, Robert De Niro, Burt Reynolds, Clint Eastwood, Barbra Streisand, Paul Newman, and a few others are frequently in receipt of scripts with multi-million dollar firm offers attached. It is highly likely that a star of this magnitude would read a piece of material with firm dates and big fees attendant to it before he would a piece of material with no offer attached. It is always good business for the producer to temper personal enthusiasm with a little realism and not wait months for Robert Redford to get to his script.

If an agent becomes a champion of your project and puts his weight behind the sales effort to get financing, it shouldn't preclude a lawyer also being involved with negotiations. Typically, agents do the groundwork and try to match up projects and buyers. They may also negotiate the highlights of a deal, such as the compensation, the term of employment, and the credits for the creative team. At this juncture, an attorney will step in to reduce the deal to writing and to negotiate the rest of the points at issue. In this way, the attorney and the agent both support the producer and work together on his behalf.

Agents and attorneys also dovetail in another important respect. Most studios or other financing entities will not accept unsolicited submissions except when made by either an attorney or an agent. This policy stems from the financiers' desire to avoid the litigation that all too frequently follows the submission of unsolicited material. There have been so many claims of copyright infringement or misappropriation of ideas by litigious submitters of material that studios have simply closed the door to them. Experience has shown that submissions that are made under the auspices of an attorney or an agent are far less likely to result in litigation.

Perhaps nothing succeeds with an agent like persistence. Agents are busy people and the bigger the agency, the more client responsibilities and the more frantic their pace. The advice always given sales people not to take rejections personally is particularly apt in dealing with agents. Stay on the case until you are able to get your message across. Be resourceful in getting to the agent and right to the point when you do. Keep in mind his problems and try to leave room in your proposal to accommodate them. Most of all, be persistent. Agents are used to receiving many calls before someone finally connects. As mentioned before, the agent's secretary can be of inestimable importance in facilitating the conversation you want. Don't ignore that fact.

While the agency business always has its share of *wunderkinds,* there has never been a particular emphasis on youth. The studio head may anticipate an average job tenure of two years, but agents can ply their trade until they see fit to retire. Personnel at the studios come and go, the fortunes of the movie industry rise and fall, and still the agent remains a fixture in the process.

3

The Studio

Even with numerous personnel changes, ownership shifts from private to public hands and back again, and financiers who arrive and depart, the studios still represent the mainstream of American picture-making and remain the principal source for obtaining funds for the production and distribution of theatrical motion pictures. They are also a surprisingly hard nut for the new producer to crack. Without the benefit of a track record or imposing credentials, the new producer understandably complains that he is given short shrift by the studios. Many independently financed films owe their very existence to their producer's inability to get a fair hearing at the studios. Much of the difficulty associated with studios arises from an insufficient understanding of the policies at work at a studio and the executives that implement them.

The major studios were originally construed to be Columbia, Warner Bros., Universal, 20th Century-Fox, M-G-M, Paramount, United Artists, and Disney. What they all shared, together with the financing of films, were divisions that also distributed films. Over the years, companies such as AIP and Filmways have entered the financing-distribution circle and then dropped out. Others such as newly formed Tri-Star, Orion, and Embassy have recently joined the fold.

The so-called mini-majors are the group of companies that finance motion pictures but distribute them through other companies. Organizations such as Lorimar, Kings Road, and Silver Screen are included in this category.

STUDIO HISTORY

The major studios of yesterday were quite different from those of today. Operating in an era before the "Consent Decrees" when the Justice Department forced the majors to divest themselves of the movie theatres they owned, the studios were an efficient means of bringing movie magic to millions of patrons the world over. The studios possessed the real estate on which vast sound stages were built and service departments, from draperies to costumes, were installed, together with contracts with all the creative talent, from producers to actors, necessary to craft movies. The films would be cranked out—some wonderful, most awful—and moved immediately into distribution in the studio-owned theatre chains.

Today, while some studios still own physical plants, others do not. Contractual relationships with talent are more the exception than the rule. Most talent operates on a free-lance basis today, moving from studio to studio depending on the particular project. While the arrangements have changed somewhat in recent years, the principal functions of the studio remain the same. They are still responsible for the making and marketing of the majority of the feature films produced in America.

STUDIO HIERARCHY

Studios, like most businesses, have a basically triangular hierarchy, with a broad base ascending to a pinnacle at the top.

At the bottom of the totem pole is the *reader*. Sometimes working out of a union and sometimes on a free-lance basis, the reader is given books, screenplays, plays, and treatments to "cover" for production executives. While the form of "coverage" may vary slightly from studio to studio, the essential content remains the same. The reader will be asked to synopsize the story, describing plot and characters in no more than a few pages.

He may also be asked to highlight the period of the story, the theme of the work, and finally his evaluation of its potential as a film. All readers have certain biases and most executives who give material to them will take this into account. If the reader's report is negative, the chances are that no one else in the studio will sample this material again. More often than not, a rejection letter will come from a production executive and will quote freely from the reader's report as the executive probably has not read the material himself.

Directly above the reader is a *story editor*. In earlier days, the story editor played a vital part in the development process. He cultivated relationships with screenwriters and novelists and worked in close collaboration with them in the further development of their work. Many writers were under contract to the studios and the story editor was in the thick of the action. Today, most story departments are more a ministerial service to the production department of the studio. The story editor serves as much in an administrative capacity as in a creative one. He supervises the readers and the dissemination of their reports, offers comments on work in development at the studio, and submits suggestions of writers or directors for projects under consideration. The story editor's efforts tend to be advisory in nature, and he is usually quite far removed from being able to say "yes" to a development situation. Nonetheless, the story editor may be a valuable ally for the producer at a studio because his view is generally considered informed by production executives.

Above the story editor in the studio pecking order are the *production executives* or *vice presidents*, some of whom may have assistants who do virtually the same thing. Their task is to attract worthwhile material to the studio, supervise it in development, oversee it in production and postproduction, and then turn it over to the marketing department. As new material is the lifeblood of the studio machine, these executives are supposed to be out in the creative community turning up promising material and writers. They are pitched throughout the day by agents, lawyers, producers,

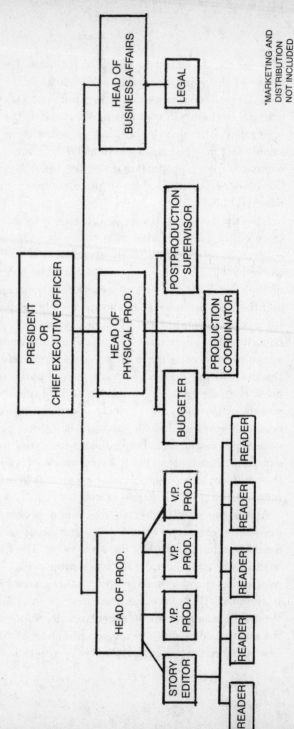

ORGANIZATION CHART
MOTION PICTURE STUDIO*

BOARD OF DIRECTORS

PRESIDENT
OR
CHIEF EXECUTIVE OFFICER

HEAD OF
BUSINESS AFFAIRS

LEGAL

HEAD OF
PHYSICAL PROD.

POSTPRODUCTION
SUPERVISOR

PRODUCTION
COORDINATOR

BUDGETER

HEAD OF PROD.

V.P.
PROD.

V.P.
PROD.

V.P.
PROD.

STORY
EDITOR

READER

READER

READER

READER

READER

READER

*MARKETING AND
DISTRIBUTION
NOT INCLUDED

and writers, all of whom have projects that they claim can be huge grossing motion pictures.

It is important to note that in addition to seeking out new projects by experienced writers, directors, and producers, somewhere in each company is an executive who is charged with the responsibility of uncovering new talent. Not only is this his primary job, but it will redound to his benefit if he can convince his colleagues that the studio should get involved with an unknown who proves later to be successful. Thus, the new producer should be selective when submitting material. He should try to enter the process at the production executive level where he will be dealing with someone who is in fact receptive to him. While it is true that most often such an executive will not be able to say "yes" to the project without taking it to a higher level, the chances are that it will get a much better reception than it would if it were submitted higher up the ladder. There is also a far better chance of having telephone calls returned and answers delivered promptly if one submits on the appropriate level. While the walls may look impregnable to the beginning producer, remember they can be breached and that inside there could be someone trying to find just such a project as the one you may have under your arm.

The *senior production executive* is known as the *head of production*. He must pick and choose among the various submitted projects and schedule their production so that the distribution people will have films to market throughout the year. While he generally has the power to approve development deals on his own, he may need approvals from those above him for certain major cash commitments or for commitments to finally finance a picture. He will frequently, as part of his administrative responsibility, assign a given project or even a submission to one of the production executives under him. It is rare that an unknown producer will have the opportunity to make a presentation to the head of production of a studio. There is not enough time in his day to hear all the proposals that sellers would like to put before him, and he must delegate a good portion of these responsibilities.

Above the head of production are a series of corporate officials whom the producer rarely comes in contact with. Their names may crop up when word filters down that a certain corporate officer has vetoed developing a project on a controversial theme such as incest or nuclear power, or killed it because he simply didn't like it. There is rarely anything that can be done in this event as corporate officers are not often willing to confront a producer on such matters. Suffice it to say that such corporate powers do lurk in the background and do have the ability, should they choose to exercise it, to scuttle even the best laid plans. Not all the people in the corporate hierarchy will figure in every piece of studio business or every development deal, which is an arrangement to further progress a project using studio funds in the hope that it will in time lead to a theatrical picture. Depending on lines of corporate authority, however, the decision to actually finance a picture may require approvals all the way up the line, often including the board of directors.

One of the great problems with understanding this operation is that so much of it happens out of the view of the producer submitting a project. He may enter the chain of authority at a comparatively low level and be greeted with unflagging enthusiasm for his submission. Suddenly, after waiting what may be an inordinately long time, he will be told that "things didn't work out," or that his contact at the studio couldn't get support when the project was discussed.

THE PROCESS OF SUBMITTING MATERIAL

Even if everything seems to have fallen into place exactly as you might have wished it, development deals and picture commitments are still subject to a variety of hurdles over which the producer has little control. Many such deals have foundered over unexpected financial shortfalls at the studio, changes in management, competitive projects at other studios, or even downturns in the economy as a whole. Clearly there is nothing you can do to anticipate most of these events. If your project goes up in flames because of such a development, you join the majority of producers who have also experienced such a result at least once in their professional lives.

What happens after your project has been left in the hands of someone at a studio is often very difficult to figure out. After it has been handed over to a reader for coverage, it will generally be delivered back to the executive to whom it was submitted. From there, assuming some kind of favorable response from the reader, it may be discussed at a staff meeting to elicit an overall response, or it may be pitched to the head of production by the executive who was originally submitted the project. Whatever happens, and it will be different depending on the studio, some kind of answer will ultimately be forthcoming. By the time you, as the producer, hear from the studio, the answer may be clear, but the reasons may never be fully explained.

It should be noted that when the picture business is suffering through one of its periodic down cycles, development deals become harder to make because less and less funding is allocated by the studios to the development area. Also, when economic circumstances are difficult, there is a tendency at the studios to concentrate decision-making in the hands of a very few individuals. When the economy is on an upturn and everything appears rosy, almost any vice president of production can commit to a development deal, sometimes on the spot. In less successful times, those same vice presidents can only recommend a deal to their superiors. The producer trying to stay afloat through good times and bad must learn to roll with the punches. He should know the climate at the studios to which he submits projects, but he should also be aware of the fact that he is usually powerless to effect changes in how studio business is carried out.

If you, the producer, arrive in town with a script or a book, you should not be surprised if most studio executives shy away from meeting with you, preferring instead to have you submit the material for coverage. This is less a personal slight and more a function of a very full, pressured day. The executive would rather have a meeting only if the material has elicited a positive response from his readers. He will then familiarize himself with the material and prepare whatever questions he has for the submitter. If a project has been packaged with a director or a writer, the studio executive may wish to have them present at the meeting to gauge the extent of their enthusiasm or belief in the project.

THE "PITCH"

If you do find yourself at such a meeting, it should be regarded much like any other sales presentation. Brevity is always appreciated by the buyer. Absent unusual circumstances like animation or special effects films, the use of elaborate art work to make a point is not a very good idea. Scripts are not bought because of the art work on the cover or extensive display materials. Usually they work against the producer. One story editor carried this proposition to its utmost point when he refused to accept scripts with the title inked on the spine. He reasoned that such markings meant the script had been sitting on someone's shelf.

There is no need to prepare budgets or marketing materials for meetings with studios. Your budget will not help sell the project and it will be reworked by the studio production department should the picture ever be set up there. It is never wrong to fashion a budget for your own edification or for use in comparing the work done in this area by the studio. For the purpose of setting up a deal, however, your rough "guesstimate" of the cost of the picture will be more than enough. As for marketing materials, they will be of little or no use to you at this stage. Neither budgets nor marketing materials will assist you in closing a development deal or a deal for a picture commitment.

The preparation of extensive casting or director lists is also unnecessary. There are a handful of major stars and a fewer number of major directors who are unanimously embraced by the studios. The involvement of an actor or a director from one of these short lists can be tantamount to getting a development deal, if not a commitment, on a picture. But as far as lists of suggestions are concerned, the studios have the same lists as you do. They are not going to be overwhelmed by your list that begins with the suggestion of a Steven Spielberg or a Clint Eastwood. They already know the importance of these people. There will be plenty of time to make lists when you are officially in preproduction.

A producer's pitch at a studio meeting should be brief, enthusiastic, and upbeat. He should have researched his project thoroughly so as to be able to respond precisely to questions from a studio executive. Such questions may be directed at aspects of the story, the cost of the material, problems implicit in the film's production, or projects competitive in theme or content at other studios. While formal lists of casting ideas should not be submitted with the material, you should be able to respond to questions about casting, whether it be with stars or unknowns.

At least as important as having factual information at your fingertips is the ability to demonstrate an enthusiastic belief in the project. Studio executives are profoundly influenced by the commitment a producer manifests in his project. The producer's confidence may be the determining factor in moving an executive from a position of being on the fence to being a supporter of the project.

DEVELOPMENT

If you have been able to effect a development deal at a studio, you will have survived the initial hazards of business affairs. The decision to make a studio development deal is made by someone within the creative executive ranks. That decision is implemented by a studio business affairs official. Sometimes the creative executive will do some of the preliminary negotiation, sometimes not. In every case, the business affairs department will wrap up the terms of the deal with the producer's agent or lawyer. Usually this will be memorialized in a deal memorandum that outlines the major business terms of the deal. Many development deals get fatally bogged down at this stage over terms of the deal or the egos of the negotiators. As a producer, you should stay very close to the negotiation, using the creative executive who "made" the deal as an ally whenever he is needed. His view can sometimes override that of the business affairs negotiator for the studio and thereby advance the project forward into development.

Once a project has become a development deal, the task of the producer is to perfect the material and take the steps necessary to get the picture made. There are several schools of thought on how to achieve this end. In the best of all possible worlds, you would work closely with the production executive who is responsible for your project and together you would bring it to a "green light" or "go" position for the studio. Unfortunately, the executives at the studio will have more projects to be concerned with than just yours. Thus, it is important for you to get used to playing the role of advocate because it will characterize much of your studio experience. It will be up to you to keep studio enthusiasm high on your project and to keep it moving until it finally receives a "go."

One time-honored technique to facilitate a green light is to get the studio to overcome its traditional financial cautiousness and to spring for as much money as possible. While this practice is probably tinged with irresponsibility, the point is that you must be aggressive about pushing for your film. Studios develop anywhere from four to ten times as many projects as they finally make into movies. In this competitive situation, you have to develop skills at playing the game in order to see good things happen for your project. It is safe to say that at the studios, absent the involvement of a major star, the forward movement of your project cannot be left to chance or the optimistic hope that the studio will act in your best interest. *You* must accept the role of being the prime mover in getting your picture made. Without your efforts, the strong probability is that it will never happen.

The most important lesson to grasp about studios and their

executives is that you and your picture are but pawns in their larger game. The executives are salaried employees for whom your picture is only one project on a development sheet. They must be concerned with not only your project but also a host of other ones, not to mention whatever politics swirl around them at any given time in a studio's evolution. You therefore make a critical mistake if you assume that the smiling face across the desk from you, offering to buy lunch and to lay the groundwork for your picture, is your new best friend. The lunch will be charged against your picture, to be recouped with interest and overhead should the picture be made, and the friendly personal attitude will be in evidence only so long as it is politically expedient. I do not mean to suggest that all studio officials are not to be trusted or relied on. Rather, it is important that you measure their words carefully, understanding the context in which they are delivered. It is highly unlikely that when it comes time to crawl out on a limb for your project you will find anyone out there besides yourself. Enlist allies wherever you can find them at a studio, but do not repose all your confidence in the words of support you are given by the studio personnel. They have their own problems that you will not be aware of, and when the going gets tough, they are very likely to respond to pressures other than your own.

During the development stage, a screenwriter will be hired, sometimes to work with a director supervising his efforts. The producer will be compensated by a supervisory fee to also work with the writer during this period. The producer's fees are in the area of $10,000 to $25,000 during this time and his services will generally not be exclusive to any one development situation. As a rule, his supervisory fee will be against the total fee due him in the event the project is produced as a film. Development entails the evolution of a project through as many script stages as are necessary to bring it to the point where it is deemed ready for production. This may require successive drafts by the originally hired screenwriter, or even the retention of a new writer to undertake rewrites on the material. While the studio pays for these development stages, the decisions as to whom to hire and how much to spend are typically made in concert with the producer.

TURNAROUND

Inevitably, some projects will not make the transition from development to production. The studio will abandon its support of the project by placing it into "turnaround." This means that the producer will be given a chance to take the project to another studio so long as the original financier is repaid his investment. The producer rarely repays these sums himself. Instead, he attracts a new studio to the project and the second studio effects its own settlement with the first. Turnarounds may result from "failed" screenplays or changes in studio management or merely a waning of enthusiasm for the project. They do provide a producer with another bite at the apple, another chance to bring his project into production.

PRODUCTION

Once your project has moved along through development until it is poised for a green light, you will have to weather the difficulties of the budget and the casting processes. Here again you may be faced with realities that impact on your project but are derived from other pressures that may beset the studio. For example, the film that has always been described as being an $8 million picture may suddenly be given a $6 million ceiling. Or, the movie that was always going to be made with unknowns may now only be given a "go" if a major star is set for the leading role. These shifts in assumptions probably have little to do with you or perhaps even your project. They may well reflect other problems or pressures that the studio faces and you will have little choice but to wrestle with them as best you can. Sometimes they will have merit to them as far as your project is concerned and sometimes they will be completely off base. Whichever the case, they are the bumps and hurdles that must be overcome if the picture is to be made.

As *Capricorn One* was poised for a "go," the studio, in this case in the person of Lord Lew Grade, turned down our casting suggestion of British character actor Donald Pleasence for an important supporting role. He insisted on our using Telly Savalas, then seen weekly in the television series *Kojak.* We argued the point on creative and financial levels, but to no avail. Finally, Lord Lew revealed his logic. He was preselling the picture to an American network and using some of these funds to defray the cost of production. The addition of Telly Savalas to the cast meant that the network would up the price it was willing to pay by half a million dollars. This logic revealed, our arguments for Pleasence were immediately silenced. (Parenthetically, Savalas was nothing short of magic in the film and brought to it a dimension that the director and I had not anticipated.) Sometimes, then, for good reasons or bad, the studio turns out to be right in its policy pronouncements.

Budget discussions can be another thorny area of studio relations. You may not be aware of the financial pressures that cause the boom to be lowered on your project. Let some pictures in release start to fail, or the studio come under criticism for its financial excesses, or the lines of financing get a little shaky, or any of a myriad of other problems occur, and you may be asked to pick up the slack by cutting costs on your film. Fair? Probably not. But whoever said that making movies with someone else's money had to be fair? Somewhat off the point, but not entirely unrelated, is the moment that occurred during the filming of *Westworld* with director Michael Crichton for M-G-M. Shooting in what was meant to be a huge dome in the Sahara desert, the weather was supposed to be a constant joy. The California climate was doing just fine until one day dawned gray and grim. Not only did the weather not match our previous day's work, it also contradicted a plot point about predictable sunshine. On location, I telephoned the studio to inform them of our decision to wait a few hours to see if the clouds would burn off. A panicked production executive on the other end of the phone replied, "Our stock was down 2½ points yesterday. Shoot! Shoot!"

There will inevitably be compromise on your part in the making of a picture at a studio. If you are able to view the process with enough detachment, it will be clear that anyone putting up $10 million for a movie is entitled to some say in the project. Yet if compromises are necessary, it is important to be able to distinguish which issues are central to the film and its creative integrity and which are not. You will want to save your biggest guns for those times when your concept of the film is threatened by a studio "suggestion." There are a handful of producers who by a fierce tenacity *and* a proven track record have earned the right to keep studio people some distance from themselves and the making of their film. Everyone else must cope as well as possible with studio mandates that may impinge on areas of the production.

THE STUDIO RELATIONSHIP

It is perhaps easier to deal with such problems if you have an understanding of the dynamic at work in such exchanges with studio personnel. They are paid a great deal of money to supervise production at their studios. Over the years, United Artists, alone among the major studios, developed a reputation for leaving filmmakers alone to make the kind of movies they wished. (And that policy finally resulted in the incredible expenditures of *Heaven's Gate*.) All the other studios, to a greater or lesser degree, saw fit to have their executives involved in the productions that they financed. This places a curious pressure on the studio executive to do his job, to handle the politics of his position, and to still let the filmmakers make their movie. Their tasks are complicated by the fact that inevitably, as projects move into production, they begin to know less and less about the projects they are supervising. As more production problems surface and are dealt with in the ordinary course by the people working on the picture, a history is written of which the studio executive has only the dimmest awareness. This is as it should be, but it does heighten the difficulty the executive may have in knowing where and how to make his presence felt.

A parent-child psychological model may be helpful in understanding the dynamic of the studio relationship. Initially, and quite understandably, the producer often sees himself as the child and the studio as the parent. The process encourages this by making the producer go to the studio for money, approvals of casting and directors, and a host of other matters, from locations to logistics. And yet, the roles are, on another plane of reality, reversed. The studio executive wants desperately to be reassured that everything is going to be all right, that the schedule and budget are going to be adhered to, and that he will not be criticized for letting the film get out of hand. Most of all, he hopes the film will succeed and that he will be able to bask in the credit always surrounding a successful film. These anxieties offer the producer an opportunity to assume the role of parent for himself. He will still have to obey the mandates of the system such as obtaining the necessary approvals, but the dynamic of his relations with the studio will change. In a word, by asserting himself in a way that allays studio anxieties, he can subtly assume the parental role and thus facilitate, to no small degree, his efforts on behalf of his project.

Conceptually, the producer and the studio should be staunch allies. The producer should have one foot firmly planted in the creative camp, with the other rooted in the school espousing fiscal responsibility. In practice, this logical order tends to break down under pressures from all sides. Too often producers are not plugged into the realities of the production difficulties of their films. Too frequently, as well, the studio executive in charge of a project is asked to convey a studio policy that is not related to the film at hand but which clearly impacts on it. These problems come under the heading of both sides doing their job. When this kind of impasse is created, tempers get frayed and the process becomes a power struggle in which the group with the most muscle carries the day. This is much less desirable than finding some means to structure a collaboration where both sides can work with a healthy respect for the other.

It should be noted that it is by no means clear that a film given virtually unlimited days to shoot and dollars to spend will be qualitatively better than a film produced under difficult financial circumstances. Tight schedules and budgets have a way of tapping into wellsprings of creativity and frequently lead to far better pictures than their plushly financed counterparts. If possible, some kind of golden mean should be achieved. The studio will try to get the best film possible for the cheapest price. The producer, in concert with the director, will seek to obtain adequate financing to implement their visions. Both sides should have a respect for the other's position and should strive to balance the equities. It makes as little sense for the studio to arrive at an arbitrary budget ceiling as it does for the producer to always want additional funding. It will always be a balancing act, and the more skilled the performers, the better the opportunity for a meaningful collaboration and ultimately a fine film.

Having argued for understanding the studio's position and seeking realistic compromises, I feel constrained to add that the effective producers of today also know when it is incumbent on them to go to the mat and slug it out in earnest. It is frequently a most difficult task to get a studio policy pronouncement reversed and it takes considerable energy and strength to accomplish it. Where you feel that it has to be done, there is very often no way to accomplish it other than to take off the gloves and wade into the fight. Many producers enjoy this, although an equal number find it a most unpleasant part of their job. But when it has to be done, you do the picture a disservice by not doing it. Some producers have been known to leap on an executive's desk, begin throwing his papers about the room, and screaming in a way that sends secretaries scurrying for cover. Everyone must do battle in his own style, keeping in mind at all times the objective of the struggle. It is all too easy to lose sight of the objective and wage pitched battle over ego needs instead. What is most important is what is right for the picture. This standard should dictate when you compromise and when you fight to the bitter end.

The battle does not end with the completion of principal photography. In the minds of many, that is where the real action starts. The studio's role in the marketing of motion pictures is the subject of subsequent chapters. Suffice it to say at this point that there will be inevitable disagreements between producer and studio as the problems of production give way to the problems of distribution.

COLLABORATION: AN ALTERNATIVE APPROACH

This chapter has focused on the new producer trying to scale the walls of a studio for the first time. There is another way to go and that is to ally yourself with an already established producer who has an ongoing relationship with a studio. While this may reduce your share of the producer's pie, it at least will allow you to sit at the table and eat your pie with the others. One of the great success stories of recent motion picture history sprang out of just such an association. That involved the teaming of Gene Kirkwood, an inexperienced producer, with Bob Chartoff and Irwin Winkler, a veteran producing team that had a relationship with United Artists. This collaboration resulted in United Artists' reluctant financing of *Rocky*, the emergence of Sylvester Stallone as a superstar, and one of the great chapters of commercial success the picture business has ever seen. Kirkwood got his picture made by piggybacking an existing relationship with a studio and went on in concert with Howard Koch, Jr., to become an important producer in his own right. Chartoff and Winkler, for their part, were able to reap greater profits than they had earned in all their previous movies put together.

It may well be easier to gain access to an established producer than it is to a studio. Since studios treat everyone equally, but some more equally than others, this may be a fruitful road to pursue. It is most important to get your foot in the door and become a part of the process. You should not despair over giving up a significant portion of the spoils if you are able to accomplish your primary goal.

The studio is the best umbrella known to the movie business when it comes to furnishing the support mechanisms necessary to produce a motion picture. From providing financing, to insurance coverage, to guarantees of completion, to the full range of production services furnished, the studio can make the producer's life comparatively easy on a logistical level. It is a privilege that you pay handsomely for, however. As will be discussed at greater length in the chapters concentrating on production, services at your disposal at a studio are very costly. It is a matter of tradeoffs. It is easier to mount a film under studio auspices, but it is unquestionably more expensive than it would be renting facilities elsewhere. The greatest advantage, in the final analysis, has to be that when the studio finally does say "yes" to your project, the odds overwhelmingly favor their having the money to see your film through. Too often with financing outside the studios, some piece of the financing will fall out at the last moment. The studio system may be an imperfect one, but it is, at the moment, better than anything else that has been devised.

4

Alternative Sources of Financing

When a producer has been turned down by the studios on a film project, or is trying to find financing for a project that is outside of the range of studio interests, he will have to look to alternative sources of financing. Perhaps his project is deemed too "small" or too "soft." Perhaps the project is a western at a time when studio wisdom has it that westerns are no longer a good financial risk. Or perhaps the project is an arty film with very limited commercial prospects. To get such films produced, or financed, the producer must come up with monies from other than studio sources because these films will probably not find their way on to a studio production slate.

THE CLIMATE

In motion pictures, as in any other business, it is preferable to deal with professionals. Professionals know the risks attendant to movie-making as well as the possibilities for critical and financial success. One of the most difficult problems of raising money outside of the studios is that very often the producer will encounter individuals drawn to the glamour or excitement of the picture business more than to the hard realities of motion picture financing.

Scratch a producer who has raised money in the world outside of studio financing and he will bleed a collection of horror stories. Independent movie financing seems to attract a rogues' gallery of fast talkers who take producers up to the starting line, and even beyond, before finally pulling the plug on their promised cash flow. And yet, many films are independently financed each year,

47

and there are numbers of producers who can recount stories of creative autonomy and financial reward attractive enough to encourage others to follow in their footsteps.

MAKING THE CHOICE: STUDIO OR INDEPENDENT

The primary question facing a producer with a project that lacks financing is whether it should be taken to the studios, or whether it stands more of a chance in the world of independent financing. There are several ways to look at this question. If you have all your money locked up from one reliable source, it is almost always preferable to go independent. By making a picture with independent, or nonstudio funds, the producer will enjoy more creative autonomy, will probably be able to produce the picture for less money, and will have a real opportunity to realize meaningful revenues from the ultimate distribution of the movie. Most producers, even if very experienced, rarely find themselves in this enviable position.

Creative autonomy comes from not having studio executives or department heads looking over your shoulder throughout the production of your film. Working outside of a studio also affords the producer important cash savings in the production of the movie. Choices of whether to use union or nonunion personnel, whether to shoot on location or on sound stages, and which people to hire for the cast and crew are all decisions that may have dramatic financial consequences. They are all decisions in which studios traditionally take an active role. It can be a blessing for the producer seeking to reduce costs to be able to make these decisions on his own.

As far as being able to realize more revenue from the film's distribution, this is normally a function of being able to make a different sort of distribution deal. Under the standard studio arrangement, the studio puts up all the money to finance the picture and to market it. For a picture to "break even" or reach a level where net profits come into play, it must earn back the

cost of production (plus interest), the cost of all prints and
advertising, and any overhead fees that the studio may impose.
In addition, the studio will subject any monies the picture earns
to a distribution fee (anywhere from 25 percent to 50 percent of
the revenues earned) which will continue even after the film has
broken even. As a rule, a studio picture must earn somewhere
between three and seven times its cost before it will reach
profitability. Thus a movie that costs $10 million to produce may
not break even until it has earned $70 million. Its earnings are
derived from theatrical distribution as well as distribution on
network and syndicated television, cable television, pay television,
video cassettes, and a number of special uses such as in-flight
airplane showings.

On the other hand, if a producer brings a completed, privately
financed film into the studios for distribution alone, an altogether
different arrangement can be negotiated. Instead of making a deal
for a percentage of the net profits, as described in the previous
example, the producer may be able to effect a "gross deal."
Under this arrangement, the producer receives a percentage of
every dollar the distribution company takes in in film revenues,
or film gross. All expenses or charges incurred by the distribution
company must be paid out of its share of the film gross. This
structure is simplicity itself. You have only to track one number,
the amount of revenue collected by the distributor, to compute
your share of the pie. While by no means foolproof, this arrangement does provide the producer with his best chance to see
significant returns with a successful film. If, for example, he were
able to negotiate a deal for 20 percent of the gross for his $10
million film, he would have received $14 million by the time the
film had grossed $70 million.

The film *Capricorn One* was independently financed by Lord
Grade and General Cinema Corporation. All the distribution
arrangements in the principal markets around the world were put
together on gross deals. This included the United States, which
figured to account for at least 60 percent of the film's anticipated

return. In the United States, Warner Bros. agreed to distribute the film for a percentage of its gross film revenues. Thus, the backers of *Capricorn One* did not have to incur significant costs to market the picture and could instead begin to participate virtually from the first dollar earned.

Capricorn One cost $4.8 million to produce. With necessary selling costs, interest, and miscellaneous expenses, the break-even point for the backers was $5.5 million. As producer, my percentage of net profits was derived from my backers' share. Thus, I became a profit participant as soon as the backers reached $5.5 million in receipts. Because all the theatrical distribution deals were gross deals and not net deals, the backers quickly got back their $5.5 million and the film was deemed to be in profits. Had the picture been made for a major studio instead of only being distributed by one, the studio's break-even point would have been closer to $20 million, or the difference between my receiving monies for my share of the profits and not receiving them.

NONSTUDIO FILMS

Which projects best fit the mold for nonstudio financing? In general, they are lower than average cost films that have the possibility of attracting casting that will make them acceptable to pay television and to foreign theatrical distributors. The studios are not enamored of films they characterize as "little pictures." Studios feel there is not enough box office potential in such projects, and with the cost of film marketing being what it is, they generally opt not to become involved. This creates a significant void in film product that has of recent times been filled by alternative money sources. In addition, there is always a place in the film market for some type of exploitation film. These might be horror, kung fu, or auto race films. Although the public traditionally responds well to such films, the studios generally shy away from financing them, and therefore these types of films may be considered good candidates for alternative financing.

ALTERNATIVE FINANCING: OPTIONS

If the choice is made to pursue independent financing, a strategy to come up with the necessary funding has to be formulated. In today's market, the financing can be viewed as pieces for an elaborate jigsaw puzzle. Each piece is a right to use the film in some medium, whether it be theatrically, on some form of television, or on video cassette. To raise money, these rights can be presold and the proceeds then can be used to make the film itself.

PREBUYS

Some of these funding sources are only cyclically in the marketplace as active buyers, most particularly network television. There have been times in recent years when the networks were very inclined to prebuy the television rights to films based only on a script, a director, and a cast. The networks reasoned that they could thus obtain a major film for a smaller fee than they would have to pay after the film's release. Many a producer was happy to go along with this thinking because it provided funds necessary to make the film, and it removed the risk of the film's not making a network sale if it failed at the theatrical box office. Today, on the other hand, the networks are less inclined to buy theatrical films before production, preferring to make their own original movies for television. The cost is less and the ratings results are better.

Prebuys are far more commonplace today from the big pay television companies such as Home Box Office. These firms will advance significant dollars to line up exclusive product for their respective systems. Along with pay television prebuys, the recent upsurge in video cassette sales has led to a corresponding increase in prebuying video cassette rights. Where only a few years ago these rights were worth very little, today it is not unusual to find companies willing to advance seven-figure sums to prebuy these rights.

The other major component in this form of motion picture financing is the selling of rights to foreign theatrical distribution. Not all projects are ideal candidates for foreign distribution. Classically, an action-adventure subject that is cast with people who are recognizable to the rest of the world outside America is the ideal project. The foreign market is evolving so quickly, however, that without considerable experience in this area, you are advised to seek the counsel of a good foreign sales representative. There are numerous such representatives or companies whose business it is to sell off the territories around the world on an individual basis. A foreign sales rep can give you a very quick reading as to whether a project is viable in the foreign marketplace. He won't want to waste time on projects he can't sell. In general, a foreign rep's judgment is a pretty reliable gauge of the acceptance level for your project in foreign markets.

Thus, the producer putting a film together outside of studio auspices will have to become skilled in the art of "creative financing." By preselling domestic or foreign theatrical distribution rights, or rights to pay television or video cassettes, he can raise the necessary funds to make his picture. The use of the unsold rights, together with any additional overages that might be due him from the successful exploitation of presold rights, constitute his hope for profits under this method of financing.

To arrange prebuy financing, the producer must assemble a package for the review of potential sources of financing. Included in that package should be a completed script, the commitments of a director, at least one member of the principal cast, a budget, and a guarantee of completion from an acceptable bonding company. A guarantee of completion is a form of insurance policy in which the insuring or bonding company agrees to put up all sums required to finish the picture above a negotiated budget ceiling. They do this in return for the payment of a premium, after a close examination of the budget, shooting schedule, and locations, as well as the experience of the people involved. Ordinarily, in a studio picture, the studio self-insures the overages that might be incurred without recourse to an outside company. In a nonstudio situation, however, the guarantee of completion is an essential element of a package as it assures the backers that the picture will be completed no matter what unanticipated problems arise.

Building into a package a director and a principal cast can prove most difficult for the new producer. By availing himself of personal contacts or using the services of motion picture agents, the producer may get his script read and even approved by a director and by an actor. Such approvals are designated "commitments." Yet implicit in these commitments is that they will stay in place only so long as the director or actor remains available. Thus, if he receives a firm offer to participate in another project, the strong likelihood is that he will feel constrained to accept it. This fact highlights the difficulty of packaging projects without the ability to close deals by guaranteeing agreed upon salaries. It is a problem endemic to the producing business. In this sense, the producer is like a juggler trying to keep a number of balls up in the air. If an actor takes another picture, one ball falls to the ground and must be replaced by another ball. It takes considerable skill to juggle everything long enough to bring the package to fruition by raising the necessary funds to cement all the deals.

Over the years, agents have been told all the possible variations of the same basic story: They should wait just a little bit longer and then all the money will be in place. At a certain point, the agent and his client will have no recourse but to insist that a firm offer be made, and perhaps that the money behind the offer be placed in an escrow account so that the agent and client know that it is there. If this cannot be done, the package will begin to fall apart.

Arlene Sellers and Alex Winitsky have put numerous projects together by going the nonstudio route. It is therefore useful to follow their strategic steps in one such effort. As a lawyer, Sellers had represented a well-known writer, Julie Epstein. Epstein had

optioned a German best-seller called *Cross of Iron* which he
adapted into a play, *Sgt. Steiner.* For various reasons, the play
was never produced, and Epstein, in turn, adapted the play into
a screenplay. Through her relationship with Epstein, Sellers had
an opportunity to see the screenplay, now titled *Cross of Iron*,
before the studios or other financing interests. She and her partner
optioned the work and set out to put their financing in place.

The first element they pursued was the director Sam Peckinpah.
Peckinpah commanded a huge following in the foreign markets
based on his action pictures. He turned out to be most enthusiastic
about the project and became the cornerstone for all future moves
made by Sellers. Using Peckinpah's commitment as the big in-
ducement, she obtained additional commitments from actors Max
Schell and James Coburn. Although both actors were known to
her personally, they could have been as readily approached
through their agents. Peckinpah was a calculated risk in this
package because of his reputation for going over budget and his
well-known irascibility. Wearing her business hat, Sellers decided
that the risks were justified because Peckinpah would provide the
means to get the picture off the ground. Results proved her
correct.

With Peckinpah, Schell, and Coburn in tow, Sellers offered the
picture to EMI for foreign distribution. They were delighted to
put up half of the budget in return for foreign distribution rights.
The action-adventure format ideally suited their needs, and Peckinpah was, for them, a vitally important director. As she had
surmised, Sellers discovered that Peckinpah was the element that
made the project viable for EMI. The fact that the underlying
work had its own following in Germany was a nice bonus in the
deal for EMI and further persuaded them to come on board.

The remaining 50 percent of the financing was put up by a
source that is not financing films today, General Cinema Corporation, one of the nation's largest theatre chains and soft-drink
bottlers. General Cinema saw merit in coming into this arrangement
because the package was appealing to them and half of the money

was already in place. As conceived by Sellers, her real money would be derived from the exploitation of the television rights to *Cross of Iron*. What she hadn't counted on was that Peckinpah built so much violence into the film that it turned out to be unacceptable for network television. Ultimately, the picture was completely recut and reassembled in order to effectuate a network sale. Likewise, Sellers was careless, by her own admission, in not accurately anticipating the economic possibilities of cable television. As a consequence, although these rights were finally sold off, they did not yield the amounts they should have.

Still in all, the picture was financed, did very well in the foreign markets, and passably well in America. All the financial backers saw some return on their money and the film is remembered as a financial, if not a critical, success.

Cross of Iron was financed because of the suitability of the script for foreign markets, the track record of the producers, and the attractiveness of the package. Frequently, the nature of the screenplay you have developed will determine where you should go first for financing. In addition to action-adventure, the foreign market historically gravitates to love stories, films with visual impact, or films rich in human emotion. Comedies, unless pure slapstick, musicals, and films that emphasize dialogue usually don't make the transition to foreign markets very well. Pay television will have its own priorities as to subject matter and creative elements. They are in such a transitional period that it is difficult to pin them down. It is always easier to effect a sale, however, when you approach the buyer with what he is looking for. You should never let any meeting with a financier in the nonstudio field conclude without asking a few questions about what kinds of things they are looking for, and what kinds of names are exciting to them. Current information is critical in this game, and the more you have, the better your chances in the marketplace.

PRIVATE FINANCING

Not to be overlooked in this process is the possibility of attracting investment money without the need of giving up any distribution rights. Whether from wealthy relatives, or other venture capital sources, such funding is an investment in a film in return for a percentage of the film's profits. Obviously this leaves the producer in the very favorable position of obtaining his funding while leaving his distribution rights intact as potential revenue sources.

In the alternative financing field, more time is spent unsuccessfully soliciting funds from private individuals than in any other single pursuit. Everyone is interested in show business, and as someone once said, the movie business is everyone's second business. Businessmen and wealthy relatives alike delight in reviewing a proposal for the financing of a film, but rarely, very rarely, will they prove willing to sign a check for the large amounts necessary to finance a film. With increments in the millions in the movie business, the effects of failure can be disastrous. Many times the producer has "sold" the private investor only to be shot down at the closing by accountants and lawyers who see their role as protecting the investor against the excesses of his enthusiasm. Sometimes, investment funds from doctors or dentists may be tapped for investment in films. Ironically, it is often the neophyte producer operating other than in New York or Los Angeles who comes up with these funds. As a rule, some tax shelter benefit is promised, and on occasion a picture is produced. If the resulting film is distributed, it will probably be under the auspices of a second-rate distributor, and everyone involved stands a good chance of losing his money. Once in a great while a film like *Texas Chainsaw Massacre* will emerge as a high-grossing picture, but will in turn be surrounded by a host of lawsuits as the parties involved scramble for the fruits of their investment. Rarer still is the quality film such as *One*

Flew Over the Cuckoo's Nest which is privately financed, successfully distributed, and proves a financial bonanza to everyone
involved. Undoubtedly, most first films in the $100,000 to
$300,000 budget range are financed by family and friends. Once
the budgets move up the scale and the stakes increase, the
likelihood of finding financing through these channels becomes
more and more remote.

SOURCES FOR FINANCING

The list of potential backers of motion pictures is a constantly
changing one. At any given time, there may be anywhere from
fifteen to thirty potential sources for multi-million dollar investments in films. The makeup of this list is in constant flux as new
money enters the marketplace and other funding dries up. Current
information as well as contacts can best be obtained from the
major talent agencies and the principal motion picture attorneys
in New York and Los Angeles. Unless the new producer is
fortunate enough to secure his financing quickly from a single
source, he will be obligated to avail himself of the services of a
first-rate agent or attorney if he realistically hopes for success in
his venture. The agent or attorney can be of inestimable help in
packaging the film and using his credibility to aid in closing the
financial deals. In consideration for these efforts, the producer
may be asked to pay some form of commission or packaging fee.
While this could run into a sizable sum, it is generally thought
to be a small enough price to pay if it leads to the movie's
being made.

An analysis of the sources of alternative financing reveals a
changing set of players around a high-risk, high-stakes poker
table. If initial investments prove successful, the players are
inclined to put up more money and stay in the game. If, as is
more likely, their investments prove unsuccessful, the tendency
of the new players is to get up from the table and retire from the
game. The truth is that without some compelling reason other

than a love of movies, there are better places for investors to put their money than in independently financed films. The currently prevailing assumption is that the need of cable companies and video cassette companies for product is just such a compelling reason. Observers of the industry therefore believe that the next important infusion of funds into the marketplace will be from these companies. New funding is always welcome and these companies hold out the hope of being in the business for some time to come.

CO-FINANCING

Many times a producer will be able to raise partial financing for his film. Rather than abandon the project at this juncture, it may be possible to approach the studios with a co-financing proposal. It is safe to say that at any given time there will be at least one studio that would welcome a co-financing arrangement. With the risk substantially reduced by virtue of having a financial partner, many studios will see fit to reexamine even those projects they have previously rejected. Partial financing is also an attractive situation for the so-called mini-majors, or those companies that have recently joined the list of motion picture financiers.

There are both federal and state laws that regulate attempts to raise money from the public. Moreover, federal and state prosecutors have shown great enthusiasm for proceeding against alleged violators of these statutory prohibitions. The distinctions between raising money privately and raising it publicly go beyond the purview of this chapter and fall into the province of attorneys familiar with this area of the law. Producers setting out to raise money must be familiar with the fact that there are statutes in this area and guidelines to be followed. Some preliminary guidance from a qualified attorney will prove of great assistance to the inexperienced fund raiser.

If you have sized up the marketplace and evaluated the relative strength of your project, there is every reason to pursue alternative sources of financing. Your campaign should be aided wherever possible by representative agents or lawyers, or both. With their help, and with a good measure of luck, you may well see your financing successfully completed and then enjoy the creative and business benefits of an alternatively financed motion picture.

5

Hiring and Working with a Writer

It is fundamental to motion pictures that everything begins with the written word. An idea may spring up in a number of ways, but a movie begins to take shape when words are put on paper. The choices that are made in the initial stages of the progression of an idea, novel, or a play into a screenplay must be lived with for the duration of the project. It is rare that unsolved problems at the script stage are successfully resolved during production or postproduction. Central to the creation of a successful screenplay is, of course, the screenwriter. Selecting a writer is one of the producer's most significant responsibilities in the evolution of a film.

Writer-director Peter Hyams, with whom I made two films, *Capricorn One* and *Hanover Street,* knows well the importance of the script. "I only know that when you put a movie together, when the film has been cut and scored and you have spliced together all of the soaring performances you can gather up, what you always wind up with is the script. In fact, the questions that are asked after people see a movie are never 'Were you using a 150mm lens?' The questions always are, 'Why didn't the guy make the phone call when he knew someone had broken into the house?' The more I work, the more I tend to see that ultimately everything rests or fails on the credibility of the story."

Many beginning directors believe they can compensate for script deficiencies with cleverness and fancy camera work. This rarely pays off. There is no shortcut to working out whatever problems exist in the screenplay before production begins. Such problems are almost never resolved during the shooting of a

60

picture. As Hyams puts it, "You would expect a dolly grip to say that the single most important part of a movie is how smoothly the dolly moves. I can tell you as a director the most important thing is the screenplay. And I learned it the hard way."

HIRING A WRITER

The sensible approach to hiring a writer is to first narrow the possible writers, from the legions plying their craft, to a manageable list of real choices. Assistance in drawing up such a list is available from several sources. You should get in the habit of noting the screenwriter's credit on movies, especially when you are favorably impressed with his work. Likewise, television credits should be closely watched in order to discover writing abilities that seem extraordinary. The Writer's Guild of America publishes a moderately priced list of writing credits which is kept current with yearly supplements. The Academy of Motion Picture Arts and Sciences and the Academy of Television Arts and Sciences, both in Los Angeles, also publish annual credits which are an efficient aid in recalling who has written which film.

The specific needs of your project must be carefully considered in compiling a list of names. Clearly some writers are better suited to one kind of film than to another. Some writers excel in action scripts, others in character studies, others in period pieces, and so on.

Help in pairing the writer and a project can be obtained from literary agents whose job it is to broker such marriages between material and writer. A description of your project's needs will generally produce one or more suggestions from a literary agent as to clients that would be right for the material. It is never a disgrace to confess to the agent that you are not familiar with a certain author's work. The agent will be more than pleased to provide a writing sample for you.

One must quickly come to grips with the problem of who is to pay the writer. If the producer is self-financing, the experienced producer will have already narrowed his list to those writers he can afford to hire. The inexperienced producer, however, cannot be expected to know the cost of the screenwriters he tentatively selects for his list. The range can be anything from less than $15,000 to $1 million, and this factor alone may control the producer's selection. If a studio or third-party money source is footing the bills at this stage, guidance should be sought as to how much the financing party wishes to spend. If the money is your own, realistic ceilings have to be set and in turn communicated to the agents in the community.

It is considered professional practice to ask an agent what his client's last several deals were and with whom they were made. These figures should be confirmed with the party who actually paid the writer. This provides a check on the agent's representations and tends to eliminate the practice of inaccurate quotations. As studios customarily won't give out prices to producers, one may need to go through a lawyer to get a confirmation of a writer's deal. This is commonly done and is considered good business practice rather than a reflection on the agent's honesty.

WRITERS

Many call themselves writers. Arguably, all this requires is a box of Eaton's Corrasable Bond and a typewriter. This may be a very appealing label, since by definition it makes the individual sound intelligent and artistic. It can sustain as an effective image only until it is time to deliver pages. Then whether one is truly a writer will be painfully apparent. In the final analysis, the single most important credential a writer can have is what he has already written. There is no shortcut to taking the time to read and familiarize yourself with a writer's work. Strengths and weaknesses are thus revealed and you will have a good idea of what to expect from the writer.

By pursuing all these avenues of inquiry, the producer should be able to fashion a list of appropriate and affordable writers. In working with each writer's agent, the final preliminary can be dealt with—availability. Your needs have to be juxtaposed against the writer's availability to determine who will be included in the final working list. Once that list is drawn, selection of a writer can begin in earnest.

MEETINGS WITH WRITERS

Many writers may be hired at this stage simply because the producer is familiar with their work. In other situations, the producer may wish to set up a meeting with the writer to hear first hand how the writer feels about the project in question. Again, utilizing an agent as a go-between, it may prove expedient to let the writer read the available material (novel, treatment, etc.) prior to the meeting. Or, equally effective, the writer can be given the material to read after a preliminary meeting has established interest on both sides in the project. By dint of the many different types of personalities involved, there simply are not hard and fast rules on the conduct of a meeting with a writer.

Hyams has formed very definite opinions about meetings and material. "I find that people tend to want to meet with you before they give you material when they have doubts about its quality. I much prefer being given a piece of material and asked to read it. Then, if I am interested, I would like to meet and talk about it. That is the time to discuss what I like or don't like about the material. I, for one, prefer not to have people explain something to me before I read it. Too often I'm told, 'The last half doesn't work, but read it anyway.' That simply makes no sense. You read the material, then you sit down and talk. Otherwise, you are likely to find that meetings tend to be much more interesting than movies that come out of them."

There is room, of course, for some differences in interpretation between the writer and the producer. It is really a question of degree. Shades of difference regarding a plot point or a character are a healthy part of the creative collaboration. Yet, when these differences become too great, there is very little point in trying to compromise. If the producer sees the project as a comedy and the writer views it as a frightening horror movie, trouble lies ahead. You are likely to wind up with a terribly scary comedy or a very funny horror movie.

Caution is also advised when it comes to that special breed of writer who has become expert at the art of "giving good meetings." He can dazzle with his wit and seeming ability to identify the strengths and weaknesses of any kind of material. He is bright, quick, and smooth. In fact, he has the whole process down pat— until the time he has to deliver a screenplay. Whatever problems prevent his being able to deliver something of quality should not be your concern. Just be aware that nobody is a good writer for your purposes until they have *written* something you find of high quality. All the rest comes under the heading of social graces: nice to have around to liven up a social event, but not so appealing when you have put up money on their creative skills.

NEGOTIATIONS AND DEALMAKING

When the list of writers has finally been narrowed to a few names, a deal has to be structured. Customarily the writer will be represented by an agent or a lawyer and will not negotiate for himself. The experienced producer generally negotiates the basic terms himself, turning the drafting and follow-through work over to his attorney. Guidelines are available from knowledgeable entertainment attorneys to assist the producer in his negotiations. In addition, the Writer's Guild publishes a schedule of its minimum payments which gives the producer a jumping-off point in his conversations with the writer's representative. Scale depends on whether the film's budget exceeds $2.5 million. For a low-budget film, it is $14,247.20, while a higher budget film requires a minimum fee of $29,319.60. The structure of deals today is sufficiently complex that the unwary producer can find himself over his head in short order. In this area (as in most other negotiations having to do with the production of films), one is well-advised to use the services of an attorney experienced in motion pictures.

In general, any negotiation should be judged by how fair it is to *both* sides. If a negotiation results in a deal that is too unfair to one party, in the long run *both* parties are the losers. In a fair negotiation, both sides emerge reasonably content and a climate where constructive creative energy can flow toward the project will be created.

It should be noted that the art of dealmaking can be a highly creative pastime. Many are the situations in which remarkably ingenious solutions to difficult problems are arrived at by very creative dealmakers. One producer, for example, arrived in Los Angeles with a modest amount of backing which he hoped to use to launch an active career. Instead of applying his funds against a well-known writer's large fees, he instead developed a compensation formula with low payments in the early stages and balloon payments, including large percentages of profits, in the latter stages. This tended to convert the writer's position from one of hired hand to one of partner. Of course, the writer bore certain risks that he would not get his customary fees. But if things proceeded well, he would be rewarded with greater sums than his standard deal provided. This particular formula has worked extremely well for both the producer and the writers who have worked for him.

THE COLLABORATIVE PROCESS

Once the writer has been chosen and his deal completed, the task of developing the script can finally begin. A collaboration between writer and producer is at best a delicate process. First, the fundamental parameters of the project have to be defined and clearly understood by both writer and producer. Second, the writer must be given enough room to explore solutions to the inevitable plot and character problems that crop up as the script evolves. How and when the producer inserts himself into this process is a matter of individual work preference, tempered by the specific writer and project at hand. An early issue to be settled is whether the writer will submit portions of the unfinished script or complete the entire first draft before showing any of his work.

There are no right or wrong answers to this question. Rather, it is more a matter of personal preference. I have preferred getting scripts in installments and meeting with the writer after receiving each batch of pages. If the right creative climate and sense of trust have been established, I feel that this is the most efficient way to avoid script "mistakes" which will only have to be rectified at a later time. In general, I think a writer should not go back to make revisions until he has finished the whole draft. Instead, the interim meetings should be used to sketch the direction of future work, while discussing the questionable areas in the submitted pages. Such meetings are rarely occasions for full-blown battles over story questions. They are more sessions to renew common visions of the work and to check and channel energies that are pulling in other directions. In this way, focus on the project can be preserved.

Often a writer is not open to the process of working with anyone. He may strongly resist showing any pages until the draft is finished and may, even then, be so protective of his work that he fights any suggestions for changes. Such writers literally have to be threatened with having another writer rewrite their work before they will at least discuss possible new directions. On the other hand, writers with whom I have worked like Woody Allen or Michael Crichton seem genuinely stimulated by a new approach to a problem. Their minds are open to fresh ideas and new suggestions seem to spark new outpourings of creative energy. Most writers fall somewhere between these extremes. One has to gauge how receptive a writer is to this process and tailor-make a system to best accommodate his work habits and his psychological frame of mind. The most important step along this road is being able to talk honestly with a writer when something is not working in a script. Even if the right answer continues to elude, the very fact that the writer is now rethinking the point allows for the possibility of change.

The process of collaboration between producer and writer can never be viewed as simply mechanical. There may be ego involvements, insecurities, or other psychological foibles that materially affect the process. Hyams notes that from his standpoint there are two things he looks for from a collaboration with a producer: "Ideally, the producer I work with has the intelligence and taste to know what is right or wrong in a screenplay and the sensitivity to understand the nature of the writer's ego. By that I mean that if you think you have written to the best of your ability, you have some stake in the words that appear on the page. If something isn't working, you certainly want someone with intelligence and story sense to break this news to you. If you trust the person you're working with, the fact that he says something doesn't work must be given serious consideration. If he remains unconvinced after all your arguments, you must somehow or other make the necessary changes." Hyams concludes, "It comes down to those two skills. You have to be able to recognize what is wrong and be able to help fix it. And, you have to possess the ability to handle the fragility of the writer you work with. I think they are equally significant skills."

From my standpoint, in dealing with a writer like Peter Hyams, I take pains to be very clear and very precise. This requires several readings of the submitted work plus taking careful, detailed notes. On occasion, there was staunch opposition from Hyams to suggested changes. Often, he would successfully defend his approach and my objections gave way. At other times, Hyams would "take it under advisement," repair to his office, and give the matter new thought. He recalls, "I remember the horrible little notes you would bring to our meetings. That meant you took the time to think it out. We knew we were always faced with making the project better. Those Nixonian legal pads meant you had done your homework, thinking and rethinking about my writing. It was then up to me to do the same."

FIRST DRAFTS

Around sixteen weeks after the screenwriter has begun his writing, he will hand in a script bearing the legend "First Draft." Experience has shown that this term means different things to different writers. The crucial question is how "finished" the screenplay is from the writer's point of view. Some writers consciously work in looser formats, intending to go back and make cuts in subsequent drafts. Other writers tend to polish as they go and accordingly deliver far tighter drafts. This has to be considered in evaluating a writer's work. You may be forced to accept successive drafts as more and more fat is cut away. This process may be likened to the ways that different directors work. Some go for the end result from the first cry of "Action!" They tend to shoot fewer takes than directors who evolve an actor's performance by letting him feel his way through a scene. Neither approach is necessarily better (although the former certainly puts less pressure on the budget). It is probably sufficient to be aware of the fact that different writers attack the process of writing in different ways. For this reason, many a producer's despair after receiving a first draft has proven premature when the writer took his script to the next level of completion.

The task before the producer on delivery to him of a first draft is both self-evident and hugely challenging. In a word, he is charged with making the screenplay better. This mission requires a delicate combination of velvet glove and iron fist techniques. The critical concern is how to improve the screenplay without sacrificing what already works well. All too often, at this vital stage, first draft screenplays are "improved" into disasters. Sometimes this results from inducing a writer to eliminate or modify the very qualities that give his screenplay freshness and singularity.

When this occurs, it is much like seeing the air let out of a balloon. The energy behind the script simply bleeds away.

Yet changes must be made. There is no point hanging on to ideas or scenes beyond their usefulness to the project. One of the hardest disciplines to acquire is the ability to let go of a good idea that no longer works in context. Sometimes the writer is the best judge of this, but equally often he is the worst.

Occasionally in this process, in addition to being a creative collaborator, the producer will have to don a second hat as financial supervisor of the movie. Wearing this hat, he may have to direct the screenwriter to make cuts in his screenplay or to revise his approach to scenes because they will be too expensive to film. Battle sequences, elaborate car chases, complicated special effects, and other similar production headaches may be removed from the script at this stage.

Most scripts are interconnected strands of theme and plot and the disruption of one element could have a disastrous effect on other sections of the piece. Thus, a sure understanding of how the various strands are tied together is essential before attempting further refinements. On balance, then, the producer should identify the center of the screenplay and trace radial spokes out from it to see the script as a whole. The author's style must not be sacrificed to the gods of logic and construction if it results in a flat, pedestrian piece. Reducing the task to its essence, you should preserve what is good and build upon it, making certain that your suggested improvements do not vitiate the very strengths you are trying to maintain.

HANDLING DISAGREEMENTS

No matter what disagreements may exist between writer and producer, they should not be aired at the studio or financier level. Such differences should be hammered out away from the presence of persons not directly concerned with the producing of the picture. This is less a recommendation to deceive a studio and more a belief that the control of a picture should rest in the hands of the filmmakers. Disagreements between filmmakers create power vacuums that studio executives rush to fill. On the other hand, if the studio feels that it is dealing with an entity, a team that speaks with a single voice, things will function considerably smoother and control will remain where it should properly be— with the team making the movie.

Many good suggestions may be forthcoming from the studio, as well as from others. As many novelists have learned the hard way, the task of writing for the screen is better described as rewriting for the screen. Unlike a novel where a few close friends and an editor may have contributions to make to the finished work, screenplays end up incorporating suggestions from many sources. Producers, studio executives, directors, stars, budget overseers, and many others all have a bona fide stake in the words on the page. Their points of view have to be carefully examined and, where appropriate, should be incorporated into the script. When a collaboration is working well, many barriers come down. Peter Hyams commented on the process of dealing with me as producer: "My experience with you has been that we wind up identifying the areas that don't work and then really bear down on them. When two people know how to work together and are familiar with each other, they are not ashamed to offer stupid ideas. We could get in a room and start exchanging ideas, insane and otherwise. That way we can explore things that we ordinarily would have too much ego to suggest. When you can work that freely, more often than not, one of those dumb ideas does spark something terrific which in turn helps a lot."

Situations may arise where work with a given writer may become counterproductive. This may result from myriad reasons, both professional and personal. The writer may cease to provide originality and surprises and his work may become mechanical and ordinary. The writer may indeed have written himself out by exhausting all his ideas. He may also have retreated behind a veil of defensiveness over how he perceives that he and his work have been treated. Work habits or personality traits may become so disruptive that a successful collaboration is impossible. For whatever the reason, matters may reach a point where to proceed further would be a fruitless and frustrating exercise. It is then incumbent on the producer, should he still have a belief in the viability of the project, to hire another writer to do a rewrite.

REWRITES

Rewriting is an art unto itself. Just as many writers shy away from original screenplays in favor of doing adaptations, so too there are many writers whose strength lies in rewriting. They have a gift for bringing out the best in a previous writer's work while shoring up the weaker portions and providing a necessary new spark of energy. Sometimes the rewriter's task will be even narrower. He may be called upon to punch up dialogue, add some humor, improve the love scenes, or any of a host of similar specialized tasks. Changes of this sort may be required throughout the shooting of the picture. Again, the compiling of a list of available, affordable rewriters can be effectuated by dealing with the literary agents of New York or Hollywood.

Some writers make their livings doing rewrites. Others look to supplement their earnings with a rewriting assignment. In any event, it is not difficult to compile a workable list of names and begin the process of winnowing them down. Having already explored certain areas with the original writer, it is essential to expose the proposed rewriter to both the existing screenplay and the underlying work. His assessment of the necessary work and his suggestions as to new directions to take should be weighed carefully before making a final decision. Invention without the hindrance of ego problems is the desired quality at this stage. The rewriter must preserve what is good and what works while rewriting that which falls short of the mark.

CREDITS

Fortunately, the determination of who gets what credit is not an issue that the producer must resolve. That aspect of the business of screenwriting has been reserved by the Writer's Guild for its own determination. The issue of sole versus shared credit takes on considerable importance as most writer's deals provide for additional compensation (both in dollars and percentages of net profits) depending on the credit received. To reach this determination, the Writer's Guild, through members of an Arbitration Committee, reviews all versions of a screenplay and decides who will receive credit and in what order—the first credit being considered the principal one. Appeals procedures exist for disappointed writers, and again the producer is not a part of the process. This frees the producer from the politics that would otherwise be involved in the difficult question of screen credits and allows him to work with each writer for the good of the project.

PRODUCTION

Once the final screenplay has been completed, most writers go on to their next assignment. There are situations, however, in which the writer will stay with a picture through production. Sometimes this is motivated by the writer's wish to remain involved with the project, especially if it is an original screenplay, and sometimes the director will ask for the writer's continued presence. The results of this particular collaboration, writer and director, range from beneficial to disastrous for the project. Some writers never accept the notion that their words will be changed as actors and the director wrestle with the content of the scenes. Other writers become immersed in the dynamics of the film and adapt to the ebb and flow of required changes. In some instances, writers work intimately with directors in preparing each day's work.

The challenge of improving the screenplay is an unending one. At some point it will no longer be possible to construct new sets or create new characters. Yet the foundation for the success of any film is the screenplay that is finally produced. Everything possible must be done to realize the full potential of your screenplay. Films are by their very nature collaborative efforts. The process of collaboration, especially in the tense atmosphere surrounding a movie, will inevitably produce disagreements. The one hard and fast guideline to be followed is that in disputes what is right for the film is the right answer for any question posed. This solution transcends politics, egos, power plays, and all other considerations that only obscure the fundamental issue. You can never be wrong by opting to go with what is right for the film.

II

PRODUCTION

6

Preproduction

There are many critical periods in the making of a theatrical feature film. Perhaps none is more important to the successful producing of a film than the period of preproduction. Preproduction lays the foundation for the production sequences that will follow, from the hiring of the necessary personnel to the formulation of the final budget of the picture. If production is the period in which the creative direction of the movie is realized, preproduction is the period during which the preparation for the business and financial aspects of production is accomplished. The evolution of the bottom line cost of production, together with the building of a team to bring home the picture on budget constitute the principal goals of this phase of a movie's evolution.

Preproduction begins when financing for a film is assured and funds are in place. Some pictures begin preproduction with an approximate notion of what their final cost will be and spend the better part of preproduction evolving a specific dollar amount which will appear on the final budget. Other films, generally independently financed, will enter preproduction with a hard and fast maximum budget number which cannot be exceeded. In both instances, the scope and direction of preproduction proceed along similar lines. A myriad of production decisions will be made in the creative area, while efforts will be constantly maintained to devise ways to keep expenses down and overall costs within stated guidelines.

ROLE OF THE PRODUCER

Preproduction is a time when the producer exercises wide managerial responsibilities in all facets of the production. He must shepherd the creative progress of the film in such areas as script development and casting. He must also supervise the establishment of financial parameters of the film which will be lived with by the entire unit, from the director to each crew member. Some producers have a vast background in production management and have come to be known as "line producers." They are able to summon precedents from their own experience in order to solve production problems that may crop up during this period. Other producers whose skills may lie more in financing or story development will have to avail themselves of the expertise of a production manager to get to the bottom of a production problem. They should, however, be sensitive to where such problems may lie.

In addition to overseeing the financial organization of the picture, the producer must also look to orchestrating the various personality types that comprise the crew in order to maintain a high morale and a happy work force. Again, he will be aided in this endeavor by the production manager who, in this sense, can be construed as straddling management and the labor force.

THE PRODUCTION MANAGER

Initially, if one already has a producer, a director, and a completed screenplay in place, the first task of preproduction is the hiring of a production manager, which is essential for the beginning of the process of scheduling and budgeting. Indeed, he will be instrumental in all the principal activities of preproduction with the possible exception of casting.

The production manager will initially turn his attention to breaking down the script and laying out his blueprint for the film on a production breakdown board. Such a board will contain, in cardboard strips, all the scenes in the film in the sequence they will be shot. These strips include the characters in each scene, a description and the location of each scene, whether it is day or night, interior or exterior, and any other pertinent information. Working with the director, the production manager completes the board. He is guided in this task by economic considerations such as the efficient scheduling of an actor or the prompt finishing of a location or a set. From this instrument, he is in turn able to begin the process of budgeting the picture.

Frequently it will prove necessary to have a production manager prepare a board and budget before financing is arranged or a director is hired. Production managers will free-lance this kind of work at a cost of $750 to $2,000. While the director's input will be required when serious preproduction begins, the early preparation of a board and budget will still provide the producer with valuable tools for the securing of financing.

It cannot be overemphasized that a prerequisite for an efficient preproduction period is a completed script. There will always be revisions that take place in a script (even throughout the shooting of the film). Hopefully, these changes will be in the area of dialogue rather than the relocation of action or the creation of new scenes with new locations. Scripts that do have drastic revisions made after preproduction has begun are the bane of production managers.

THE PRODUCTION DESIGNER

In most situations, after the hiring of a production manager, the next crew member to come on board will be the art director or the production designer. As his area of responsibility extends throughout the picture, this individual will have considerable say in the "look" of the film, from sets to costumes. It is imperative that his ideas for these areas mesh with those of the director and producer. The financial ground rules as to whether the film will be a low-cost or a high-cost picture must be clearly understood so that everyone is making the same kind of film.

LOCATIONS

With the production manager and production designer hired, the selection of locations can begin. If the project is to be filmed on a sound stage, little time need be spent in this area. If, however, the film is to take place on location, considerable research may be required. Only after locations are selected can specific costs begin to be compiled. The logistics of moving a 150-person crew in and out of a remote location, including the housing and feeding of them, is a major undertaking. Once locations are set, realistic costs can be determined.

TRANSPORTATION AND CONSTRUCTION

The transportation captain and the construction coordinator are two other department heads who should be hired at the time location scouting begins. Not surprisingly, these men supervise two of the most volatile accounts in the budget. Wrong guesses in their areas can produce budget errors of hundreds of thousands of dollars, and beyond. It is extremely useful to seek their advice and consultation at the planning stages of a picture. Not only can they save the production a great deal of money, but the failure to use them correctly can cost the production an enormous amount above the budget ceiling.

THE PRODUCTION SECRETARY

The last member of the early preproduction team to come on board is not a true department head, but is no less valuable. This is the production secretary. She (for most production secretaries are historically women) must function as a communicator and expeditor. Any breakdown in her job performance will create bottlenecks that will greatly impede the efficient administration of the production. Most information is disseminated through her office to department heads and other crew members. In many films, she becomes the production manager's alter ego, handling problems large and small, and keeping the picture on a straight and true course. Not only must she be aware of the problems of production, she must also be a keen student of psychology, possessed of great patience, tolerance, and managerial skills. Care should be taken in the hiring of this person because major problems lie in store for the production with an inefficient or incompetent individual in this position.

THE SHOOTING SCHEDULE

The shooting schedule is regarded by most production managers as a virtual bible for the production period. Michael Rachmil is a production manager with whom I have done three feature films and nearly seventy educational films. He is at the forefront of the young and talented production people who have emerged as industry leaders in the last decade. For Rachmil, there cannot be enough time spent on the preparation of the shooting schedule. This grows out of the fact that, if well prepared, the shooting schedule will include everything needed for a given scene from actors to props to special effects. It will be used by department heads during shooting to ensure that they are fully prepared for each scene and that there will be no time lost during production because of misunderstandings as to what the particular scene demands. An example of the detail provided by a shooting schedule may be seen in this excerpt from the *Barbarosa* schedule.

There are literally thousands of decisions, large and small, that must be made during preproduction. All aspects of the picture from hairstyles to wardrobe to props and to the technical equipment necessary to shoot the movie must be solved. Production meetings for all department heads are held on a weekly basis and

BARBAROSA SHOOTING SCHEDULE

DATE	SET/SCENES	CAST	LOCATION
9TH DAY THURSDAY 9/25/80	*EXT. MEXICAN VILLAGE* Sc. 15 Day—1/8 Pg. Arriving adrenalin reluctant employee.	KARL OTTO FLOYD *EXTRAS* 30 Extras	TERLINGUA CANTINA *PROPS* Carts Wagons *ANIMALS* Horses Goats Chickens Burros Otto's Horse Floyd's Horse *EFFECTS* Smoke *MAKEUP* Karl's Face Healed (2 weeks later)
	INT. WHORE HOUSE— SHOT FROM EXT. Sc. 16 Day—2/8 Pg. Karl pours water on whores—(2 wks. later).	KARL *EXTRAS* Old Whore Young Whore	*ANIMALS* Horses Burros Goats Chickens *MAKEUP* Whore has Evident Scar
	EXT. CANTINA Sc. 16A Day—1/8 Pg. Skulking brothers.	OTTO FLOYD *EXTRAS* Extras	TERLINGUA CANTINA
	EXT. MEXICAN VILLAGE Sc. 17 Day—1/8 Pg. Karl back up hill to cantina.	KARL	SAME AS ABOVE *ANIMALS* Horses Chickens Goats Burros *EFFECTS* Smoke
	EXT. VILLAGE— CANTINA Sc. 20 Day—1/8 Pg. Quick exit.	KARL OTTO FLOYD *EXTRAS* Whores Cantina Owner Bartender Mexican Men 3-Piece Band 30 Extras *STUNTS/ DOUBLES* St. Dbl. Karl (Ride Out)	TERLINGUA CANTINA *PROPS* Guns *ANIMALS* Horses Cast Horse for Karl— steals Mexican horse Goats Chickens Burros *EFFECTS* Smoke Bullet Efx. *MUSIC* Band Inst. as B4
	EXT. VILLAGE— CANTINA Sc. 23 Late Day—1/8 Pg. Eduardo on track.	*EXTRAS* 30 Extras Cantina Owner Whores Mexican Men	*WAGONS* Carts Wagons *ANIMALS* Eduardo's Horse Chickens Goats Horses Burros

END OF 9TH DAY—TOTAL PAGES: 7/8

are generally chaired by the director with the assistance of the production manager. In these meetings, production questions about the film are put to the director by the department heads. At the end of this process, a shooting schedule will be distributed which will include the specific requirements of each day's shooting. The grand design for preproduction is to anticipate, insofar as humanly possible, all the production needs for the picture. Should decisions not be made during this time, inevitably there will be confusion bordering on chaos during the production phase of the picture. While films have muddled through in such a state of confusion, it is never without profound impact on the budget and the quality of what appears on the screen.

DAY-OUT-OF-DAYS SCHEDULE

Upon completion of the production board, the production manager will be able to complete a day-out-of-days schedule which tells the producer when each actor works during the course of the schedule. This is of vital importance in the structuring of the actors' deals. Only if this is done with meticulous care can an economically effective cast budget be determined. Many times the shooting schedule will have to be juggled for one reason or another and this can have disastrous consequences for the cast budget. Hopefully, the actors' deals will have been made with sufficient flexibility so that the schedule can be reworked without undue negative impact upon the budget of the film. If an expensive actor is to be employed for less than the full shooting schedule, then it behooves the producer to compress his work schedule to as few weeks as possible. It will then be incumbent on the director to complete that actor's services as expeditiously as possible.

DAY OUT OF DAYS   Initial Date Issued __12/7/83__   Revision # _____

SCRIPT DATED	SCRIPT TITLE	PRODUCER
	"TROUBLE AT THE ROYAL ROSE"	
PRODUCTION #		

MONTH ————➤

	DAY OF MONTH ————➤	
DAY OF WEEK ————➤	M T W Th F S Sn	M T W Th F Th	M T W Th F S Sn
SHOOTING DAYS ————➤	1 2 3 4 5 6	7 8 9 10 11	12 13 14 15 16 17

#	NAME	CHARACTER	#
1	ARNOLD BAKER	Appleton Porter	1
2		Mona Smith	2
3		Angus Watkins	3
4		Alicia Arkwright	4
5		Harry Lewis	5
6		Jason Lock	6
7		Martha March	7
8		"Moustache" - Agent II	8
9		Maria Sola	9
10		George Trent	10
11		Unseen Woman	11
12		Capt. Domingo Sanchez	12
13		Stranger in Car	13
14		Taxi Driver - Agt. 15	14
15		German Woman	15
16		2 Skater Killers	16
17		Perry the Parrot	17
18		Dog	18
19		Cat	19
20			20
21		Special Effects	21
22		Stunts	22
23		Cars	23
24		Helicopter	24
25		Extras	25
26			26
27			27
28			28
29			29

Date Revised _____

DIRECTOR
Burt Kennedy

R: Rehearse
NCR: Non-Consecutive Rehearse
TV: Travel
S: Start
W: Work
F: Finish
H: Hold/Carry

O: Holiday
L: Loop
NCL: Non-Consecutive Loop
P: Protection Day

M T W Th F S	M T W Th F S	M T W Th	Rehearse	Travel	Work	Hold/Carry	Holiday	Loop	Protection Days	Start Date	Finish Date	TOTAL	
18 19 20 21 22 23	24 25 26 27 28 29	7 8 9 10											
W W W W W W W W	W W W W W H W W	W W W		3	34	9	1						
W W W H W H H W	W H W H H H W F			1	15	13	1						
H H H H H W H W	F			1	7	20	1						
H W W H W H H H	Tv H H H W H H H H W			1	6	28	1						
W W W H W H H H	Tv H H H H H H H H W			1	6	13							
H H H H H H H H	Tv H W H W H H A H H			2	8	28	1						
W W W H W H H H	Tv H H H H H H H H W			1	7	27	1						
H H W H W W Tv H	W W H H H W W			2	10	20	1						
W H W H W W H W	F			0	8	11	1						
H H H H H H W H	F			0	3	17	1						
H H W F				0	2	16	1						
W H H H H H H H H Tv	H H H H H H W F			1	3	19	0						
				1	2	0	0						
H H H H H H H H Tv	H H H W F			1	2	27	1						
H H H H H H H H Tv	H H H H H H W F			1	3	30	1						
W W W W H H H H Tv	H H H H H H H H W			1	7	14	0						
H H H H H H H H Tv	H H H H H W F			1	3	18	0						
				0	1	0	0						

THE BUDGET

The budget is the final product of the completion of the shooting
schedule and the production board. It normally goes through five
or six drafts before each department's final numbers are definite.
As Rachmil points out, "What I normally do is to put in a
'guesstimate' for all the department heads and then distribute the
script to each department. The department heads report back
with their respective budgets. As their budgets are usually higher
than my 'guesstimates,' I make the necessary adjustments. It is
up to me to ride herd on them and try to bring them into line. I
can usually get them to lower their figures, but then I run the
risk that they'll go over. All of this juggling is what production
management is all about."

Production management entails the establishment of certain
assumptions which will govern the course of production. Should
the picture be done on sound stages or practical locations, with
union or nonunion personnel, at a television pace (eight to ten
script pages a day) or a motion picture pace (two to four pages a
day). It is thus possible to produce a film for a cost that will vary
within a broad spectrum, depending on the assumptions made. It
is of crucial importance that the producer, director, production
manager, and financier all understand these assumptions and what
production decisions are implicit within them.

Recently technology has provided tools that are a great boon
in the area of production management. Not only has payroll
accounting shifted from manual work to automated systems, the
process of budgeting and boarding has moved to computers as
well. Utilizing programs with current salary rates and fringe
payments from all over the world, such computer programs
greatly shortcut the tedious chore of doing all this work by hand.
In the process, literally hundreds of labor-hours are saved as
different assumptions may be tested in a few minutes of computer time.

OVERAGES AND CONTINGENCIES

The uncertainties inherent in the budgeting process lead the shrewd production manager to "hide" some extra monies in the budget to cover the unpredictable overages that almost certainly will occur. If he has done his job well, he will have pushed the department heads to take the fat out of their respective budgets and will have protected himself (and the budget of the picture) against the unforeseeable. Studios used to respect the uncertainties of production by sanctioning contingencies as an integral part of every production budget. Thus, a typical budget would have a 10 percent cushion to accommodate these kinds of problems. Today, most studios do not countenance contingencies, although typically most independent pictures do. This has made budgeting something of an art because few production managers want the reputation of bringing in pictures over budget. As budgets are prepared under close studio scrutiny, the creation of "pads" is often a difficult task. Rachmil is typical of his brethren when he says that he would "rather have my fights with the financier up front, as opposed to going over budget and having my fights later." Rachmil goes on to say that studio people or others putting up the money for a film would far rather hear any bad news during the budgeting process than during production.

In preparing his budget, Rachmil pays particular attention to the construction and transportation accounts. Experience has shown him that they are the most volatile from the standpoint of going over budget. Props and set dressing often miss the budget mark, particularly on location, but the amounts involved rarely touch the potential overages from construction and transportation. Problems with construction are not hard to understand. Overly ambitious art directors are frequently guilty of paying more attention to the look of the sets and less to the production costs. Then, too, construction often proceeds ahead of the main unit of the company, a fact that permits it to function without the close supervision found in other areas of the production. As Rachmil says, "Today I'd hire a person to do nothing but watch construction costs. His job would be to tell me where we are every day."

Transportation can be abused almost as much as construction. This is frequently tied in with construction, especially when the unit is in two different places. There also seems to be no way to anticipate the need for cars when a unit reaches location. Cast and producers, husbands and wives, visiting dignitaries, and many others need cars that may not be budget items. They may also require the services of a Teamster driver which will increase labor, housing, and feeding costs as well. As Rachmil says, "A good rule of thumb is that you can never put enough money in the transportation account."

Certain films will have special accounts that have trouble written all over them. An example of such an account is special effects, which in today's films generally involve state of the art technology. This is an extremely difficult area to budget because the skilled technicians who come up with special effects wizardry are sometimes at a loss to accurately predict how long they will have to work to achieve their miracles. It is actually less a matter of how long the process will take but rather whether it will ultimately be successful in time for the film's release. On *Futureworld* we had allowed for ample time and money to prepare a computer-derived plan for a likeness of our leading man. We hired the best technicians and the best hardware company and provided them with as much time and money as seemed reasonable. As the deadline grew near, however, it became clear that the problem was not one of money but rather whether the agreed upon imagery could be achieved at all. This is more than a little disconcerting when the apparent alternative is nothing more than a "Scene Missing" card to run in the answer prints of the picture. A last minute breakthrough solved the *Futureworld* problem, but not before the budget increased dramatically to accommodate overtime for an increased number of technicians.

As indicated, a budget is divided into two principal categories, above-the-line and below-the-line. The "line" divides the so-called creative personnel—the writer, producer, director, and cast—from the "technical" personnel required physically to make the picture. While these categories are arbitrary, they have survived several decades of picture making and are in common usage. The budget is further divided into accounts which detail all the projected costs of the film. Everything from fringe benefits on salaries to the costs of car rentals will be included. For convenience, all the budget numbers are summarized on an account by account recap called a "top sheet." While the full budget with all its detail may run anywhere from fifty to ninety pages, the top sheet provides fast answers to most of the questions that may arise. It will certainly allow, at a glance, a fast reference to which accounts stand out as unusually large or in some other way disproportionate to the overall budget.

The first compilation of these numbers is prepared by the production manager, sometimes working in concert with the director. Each account's total is then turned over to the department head supervising that area. The projected figures are then tested against the realities of the marketplace and any discrepancies are reconciled. Out of this process will come a final budget which will be signed by the producer, the director, and the production manager.

THE PRODUCTION MANAGER AND THE STUDIO

Much has been made of the role of the production manager during the vital preproduction period. In many situations, he has been hired, or at least approved, by the studio or other financing source. There is always, therefore, the possibility that the production manager may feel a potential conflict of interest between the needs of the producer-director on the one hand and the studio on the other. Mike Rachmil acknowledges these sometimes competing interests by saying that, "In the end the production manager is responsible to all of these various interests. He can't

7 WEEKS LOCATION SHOOTING & 1 HOLIDAY   AUG. 29, 1984

EST. # _____   PROD # _____

WORKING TITLE

AC	DESCRIPTION	PG #		TOTAL BUDGET
00	PRODUCER'S UNIT	1	698,760	
02	DIRECTION	2	100,734	
04	STORY RIGHTS	3	182,800	
06	SCREENPLAY	3	–0–	
08	CAST	4	504,320	
	TOTAL ABOVE-THE-LINE			1,486,614
20	SET DESIGN & ART WORK	5	22,200	
22	MATTE PAINTING	7	–0–	
24	SET CONSTRUCTION & ALTERATIONS	6	64,100	
26	FULL SIZE EFX SET CONSTRUCTION	7	–0–	
27	SET DRESSING	8	34,000	
28	MINIATURES	7	–0–	
29	SET STRIKING	6	6,500	
31	PROPS. SPEC. EQUIP. & LIVESTOCK	9	49,050	
32	LIGHTING	10	84,800	
34	WARDROBE	11	37,050	
36	MAKE-UP	12	27,900	
37	SOUND PRODUCTION	13	41,391	
38	CAMERA	14	203,100	
39	TRANSPORTATION & PICTURE CARS	15	269,650	
40	EXTRAS	16	28,340	
42	SET OPERATIONS	17	198,475	
43	FILM & LABORATORY – PRODUCTION	18	120,989	
44	PRODUCTION STAFF	19	53,900	
45	SECOND UNIT PROVISION	18	40,000	

#	Description	Acct	Amount	Subtotal	Total
46	LOCATION EXPENSE	20	305,467		
47	VIDEO OPTICS PRODUCTION	21	3,500		
48	STAGE & SET RENTALS	21	7,550		
50	TESTS	21	7,500		
54	PUBLICITY	22	21,500		
55	SPECIAL UNIT	22	8,500		
58	FRINGE BENEFITS	23	110,189		
59	MISCELLANEOUS	23	239,250		
	TOTAL PRODUCTION			1,984,901	
60	PHOTOGRAPHIC EFFECTS	24	12,500		
61	FILM & LABORATORY – EDITORIAL	24	38,794		
62	EDITORIAL & PROJECTION	25	188,900		
63	VIDEO OPTICS – EDITORIAL	26	5,000		
64	STOCK SHOTS	26	750		
66	TITLES	26	15,000		
68	SOUND – POST PRODUCTION	27	126,755		
70	MUSIC	28	125,000		
78	FRINGE BENEFITS – POST PRODUCTION	28	15,610		
	TOTAL POST PRODUCTION			528,309	
	TOTAL BELOW-THE-LINE			2,513,210	
	TOTAL DIRECT COSTS				3,999,824
83	FILM FINANCE FEES	29			
84	VALUE ADDED TAX	29			
85	SPECIAL DEPOSITS	29			
89	GENERAL STUDIO OVERHEAD	29			
	TOTAL INDIRECT COSTS				
	TOTAL BUDGET				

take sides. He must be honest with everyone and call the situation as he sees it." In the studio context, it is standard procedure for a production executive to call his production department for information on a movie being shot. The production department, in most instances, will call the production manager with whom they have the most contact. Questions like how long will it be before a scene is finished, or a set wrapped, will be asked of the production manager. The answers to these queries can be guessed at by the production manager. It is an educated guess, to be sure. But the real answers to such questions inevitably lie with the director.

By staying close to the director and his thinking, the production manager will best be able to field any inquiry from the studio or any other source. If the director and producer, in turn, have any anxieties about the production manager's conversations with the studio, then they have selected the wrong man for the job. This area cries out for free and open exchanges of information, and most of all, for saying the same things to all people involved. Adds Rachmil, "That is my basic rule. There is nothing that I would say to the studio that I would not say first to the producer and the director. In short, there is a common task and there should be no hidden agendas."

As the movie moves closer to production, other members of the crew are hired and begin to play a role in the budgeting process. There is often a lively dialogue between the various department heads and the production manager in which the department heads struggle to meet their budget ceilings and/or to get more money allocated. As with the rest of today's economy, everything seems to cost too much and the pressures on the budgeting process are always focused on cutbacks and compromises. The producer must balance and reconcile the competing interests of financial necessities and creative visions.

CASTING

Nowhere is this balancing act more evident than in the casting of a film. There are numerous considerations in the casting of the principal roles of a movie. Ideally, the producer and director select the best actor for the part. In practice, such factors as recognizable names for the foreign market, budget limitations, actors' availabilities, and the inevitability that some actors will reject the part all come into play.

Casting directors are of great assistance in the casting process. Their expertise is utilized in compiling lists of actors within a given price range who would be suitable in each part. The logistics of meeting such actors, dealing with their agents, and even negotiating terms of employment are handled by casting directors and their staffs. Although a highly specialized end of the film business, casting directors can be of inestimable value to the producer in saving time and broadening the list of potential acting candidates. In general, casting directors will make recommendations to the producer and director but will not have the authority to close deals on their own. In many instances, the star of the film may be set before the casting director has begun work. In such cases, the contribution of the casting director may lie in suggesting other actors and negotiating the deals for the rest of the cast.

ACTORS' DEALS

Whether or not the casting director is involved, negotiating deals for star performers today will generally involve some discussion of percentages of the film's net profits or, in rarer cases, the film's gross receipts. Any discussion of net or gross percentage must also include the distribution company from which such payments would ultimately be forthcoming. The producer must consult with the appropriate representatives of the distributor before making commitments in this area. The advice of a lawyer is also generally recommended for such negotiations.

In the past, I have customarily negotiated the major points of star deals before turning the negotiation over to counsel to finish. The points covered in my discussion with an agent representing a star include the salary, term, billing, expenses, and any special provisions the agent invokes on behalf of his client. The precise contractual language employed is the province of the lawyers in this matter. I, as producer, would hand the attorneys a memorandum reflecting my understanding of the negotiated deal. In the process of negotiating these points, it would not be uncommon for me to check previous prices or terms of employment with the actor's previous employer. Agents' quotations can often be misleading in this regard. An example of how this operates is the "free weeks" area. If an actor is hired for ten weeks for a fee of $100,000, many agents will have the contract drafted as eight weeks plus two free weeks. By this technique, they are able to quote the actor's weekly price as $12,500 instead of $10,000. A little research goes a long way in uncovering what really went on in previous negotiations.

SELECTION OF CREW

Another aspect of preproduction which often receives short shrift in the planning stage is the selection of crew. Mention has already been made of the need to hire the production designer, the transportation captain, and the construction coordinator. But how are these individuals to be hired? And by whom? Many production managers tend to use the same key personnel in all their projects. This produces the obvious benefits of predictable performance levels coupled with the absence of bad surprises along the way. But does it also produce the best film? Rachmil, for one, has tended to move away from the notion that he and the film are best served by hiring the same people each time out. He now seeks the best person for the job, whether he or she be a veteran or a newcomer. In part this grows out of the increased budgetary pressure of recent years. In part, also, it represents a shift in emphasis from the benefits of familiarity to the advantages in finding the most qualified person for the job. Better to have someone who is truly enthusiastic about doing your film than someone who is along for the ride because he always works with a certain production team.

The hiring of crew is not a task that should be left to the production manager alone. He is, of course, a key resource in suggesting names for department heads. But the hiring process should involve the director and the producer as well. It is far better to have everyone in a room to discuss the strengths and weaknesses of crew members during the hiring process than to wait until you are all in a hotel room on location during a production crisis. In this way it is possible to avoid the negative impact of an incompetent crew member. Too little attention is paid to the mix among the personalities of the various members of the crew. How will they get along with one another? Is there a history of problems? These facts can be unearthed with a little research and can go a long way toward avoiding problems from the first day of shooting. It is important to note that like the rest of preproduction, foundations are laid for the morale of the company which will be severely tested at a later date.

PREPRODUCTION CONSIDERATIONS

Almost every film will have special problems that must be solved during preproduction. Sometimes something as particular as the consent of a craft union can pose insuperable problems for the production team. For example, the Australian director of *Barbarosa*, Fred Schepisi, wished to use his Australian cinematographer, Ian Baker, on the picture. The Los Angeles and New York Local branches of the camermen's union blocked all efforts to obtain a work permit for Baker. Although they did not deny Baker's stature within the film industry of Australia, they took the position that the work should be given to a member of their own Locals. In the case of *Barbarosa*, the Local in Chicago consented to Baker's working within its jurisdiction—an area which included Texas. So important was Baker to Schepisi's approach to *Barbarosa* that Texas was chosen as the sole location for the picture.

Much has been written about how long preproduction should last. The simple answer is as long as possible. Few are the movies that could not benefit from two or three additional weeks of preparation. Yet as a rule of thumb, it is probably more efficient to think in terms of the same number of weeks for preproduction as you have scheduled for production. You can surely do the job in less time, but the additional weeks can only serve to better construct the movie's foundation and to save time and money during production. Of course, the complexity of the film is the major consideration in arriving at the prescribed number of weeks for preproduction. All films are different and to a certain extent each requires a separate assessment for preproduction, just as it does for production. If great care is taken to make the preproduction period as efficient and productive as possible, it will pay huge dividends down the line.

7

Production

Production is the time of greatest opportunity for filmmakers. Production is also that time in a motion picture's evolution when the bulk of the cost is incurred, which means it is the time of greatest risk for the financial backers. Even with the most diligent care in preproduction, production still remains a problematic period. Such difficulties inevitably lead to the clash between the competing interests of finance and filmmaking. In the midst of this activity, the producer finds himself in a difficult and challenging position.

THE ROLE OF THE PRODUCER

Some producers tend to absent themselves from production altogether. If their film is shooting at the same studio where they have their office, the coincidence of geography may cause some contact with the unit. Yet if the unit is on location, the producer may be virtually out of touch. These producers may be in contact with the unit by telephone to allay the anxieties of the financiers, and consider themselves on call in the event of severe problems or emergencies.

Other producers find much to become involved with during a picture's production, filling a number of roles, and finding a definite place for themselves in the process of making the picture. These producers' efforts are focused on both the business and the creative aspects of the production.

From the moment shooting begins, the producer on location or on a sound stage may be involved with the production. While this may sound obvious, the difference between a producer who is always present and a producer who drops in once or twice during production is enormous. A motion picture crew is a tightly knit unit with its own power structure and organizational makeup. A producer who is not present through most of the shooting will inevitably be treated as a stranger by the crew. While courtesy and respect will still be present, the producer, from the standpoint of the crew, is simply another "biggie" who has to be driven around. If, on the other hand, the producer is an active part of the production unit, the crew will be inclined to open up to him and to reveal the operation, good and bad, of the production unit.

MANAGING THE MOVIE

MANAGING COMMUNICATION

The producer who has spent his days and nights with crews on distant locations is likely to hear scuttlebutt that may be of inestimable value in managing the production. From the first assistant director to the production manager, to the cinematographer, key members of the crew will seek out the producer to discuss their problems or problems they have observed. Often these discussions provide insights that permit the producer to improve some facet of the filmmaking process, usually in the area of efficiency.

Most crew members are motivated to turn out a quality product at an efficient and cost-effective price. Usually the key members of the crew will be extremely troubled by their observation of unprofessional behavior by the director, the stars, or their peers. As producer you should have this information but it is not easy to obtain. Clearly the crew will not impart such information to a producer who visits the set infrequently. There is, therefore, no shortcut to spending time with the crew, becoming accepted as part of the production unit, and in this way tap into the wealth of information that crew members uniquely possess. Once that relationship has been formed, it allows for an informal exchange of information. For the producer who wants to actively involve himself in the process of making a movie, there is no better way to glean the necessary information than to be there and to establish working relationships with the crew.

Fred Schepisi's unique method of shooting in *Barbarosa*, for example, created problems for the crew. Schepisi used a 1000mm lens for most of his exterior shots, which forced the camera department to work much further away from the unit than usual. Unfamiliar with this way of shooting and unused to the techniques employed by Schepisi, the crew began to develop a negative attitude. By being a constant presence on the set, I not only heard these grumblings of discontent but was able to put together an informal session at which Schepisi and the key crew members aired their concerns and put the production back on a sound footing.

Communication is of vital importance in the management of any business. Filmmaking, as a business, is no different. In addition, the pivotal crew member during production, as he was during preproduction, is the production manager. Dialogue with the production manager will provide a solid foundation for the efficient management of the business side of a film. Problems can be resolved, information can be exchanged, and strategies can be formulated for dealing with the exigencies that arise.

MANAGING PUBLICITY AND PUBLIC RELATIONS

A second important function for the producer during production is the supervision of all public relations and publicity relating to the film. Different films require different approaches toward publicity. If the film is made independently without a distribution deal, one set of requirements must be fulfilled. Films seeking distributors must disseminate a constant stream of publicity releases to create a level of interest about the film. Specialized public relations firms in New York and Los Angeles are most adept at distributing messages of this kind to appropriate film distributors in foreign countries. The producer's role in overseeing this process can be a very important one. He must personally supervise the art and the copy that describes the picture. Most copywriters, left on their own, will not do justice to the visions of the producer or the intentions of the filmmaker. If you are not careful, you will find that the world is developing a completely different impression of your film than the one intended or envisioned.

In the event that a film is already placed with domestic and foreign distributors, then the amount of information flow will probably be different. Supervision of copy and art will still be necessary, but the need to send publicity releases to local distributors will be erased. Emphasis shifts, in the latter circumstance, to orchestrating local and national press during production. In some cases, as with *Close Encounters of the Third Kind,* the filmmaker adopts the policy that no news is correct news. Shrouded in mystery, that film achieved a high level of visibility by telling people nothing. However, the more common situation is one in which the studio or other distribution company will seek some profile for the film and its principal players. This will often take the form of interviews and/or photographic essays which are generated in part by the unit publicist working on the film and in part by visiting press and special photographers. Again, the more control that the producer can exert over this process the better.

It is important to keep studio excitement about a film at a high level so that its enthusiasm will be communicated to the exhibitors and finally to the general public. The producer must assume the quarterback's role and coordinate the activities of all press, including the unit publicist, throughout the course of production. By exercising this control, offending copy can be replaced immediately. It is not enough to wait until the picture is ready to be released. By that date, materials will have been created and copy will have found its way into press releases and promotional materials. Instead, the producer must take an active role in guiding and steering all activities in this area from the moment the picture is green lighted.

MANAGING THE CAST AND THE DIRECTOR

Another area where the producer may be of major assistance in the production of a picture is in the relationship with the principal cast. While the relationship between the director and the stars must be preserved so as to get performances on the screen, the off-screen problems of the stars can often best be handled by the producer. Most directors will welcome the involvement of the producer in helping to keep the stars happy. There are few guidelines for this frequently difficult task. Suffice it to say that the ego problems that constantly arise on films have to be dealt with in a caring, understanding manner. Any time the producer is able to relieve the director of some of this responsibility, there will be more time for the director to prepare his next day's work.

The relationship with the director is such an important area of the producer's work that it warrants a separate chapter. It should be noted here, however, that a strong collaboration between producer and director can often forge a vital link in developing a successful film. This collaboration can extend from assessments of dailies to crisis management when disasters strike.

During production, the day to day process of making a movie is commonly perceived as being supervised by the director. On one level, this is true. Yet while the cast and crew turn to the director for creative instructions, in general terms the unit must turn to the producer for financial guidance. It is the producer who must ride herd on the movie's progress from a financial perspective.

MANAGING THE FINANCIAL SOURCE

Finally, the producer, in most situations, will be in close touch
with the studio or other financing source. In this respect, the
producer is responsible for keeping the studio off the director's
back, thereby freeing the director to spend his time shooting the
film. The producer has one foot in the creative area and the other
in the financial. As he straddles both spheres of interest, he
attempts to reconcile frequently competing points of view. His
success at these tasks will be a major factor in the maintenance
of quality and efficiency in the production of the film.

THE CREW IN PRODUCTION

The analogy of the producer as a manager is an apt one. If his
task is seen as analogous to that of an executive running a
company, then considerations such as crew morale will jump to
the fore. My experience in Lajitas, Texas, is a good example of
the kinds of problems that locations can pose for crew morale.

Lajitas, the principal location for *Barbarosa*, is a town on the
Texas-Mexico border with a permanent population of twelve. The
normal creature comforts provided for American crews were not
to be had in Lajitas. Instead, the crew was doubled up two to a
room, spread over a 50-mile area, and deprived, because of the
remote geographical location, of the benefits of telephones and
English language radio and television. Given these circumstances,
a major morale problem for the crew presented itself.

The answer to this kind of situation is to do the best you can.
Pool tables were rented, video cassette players secured, and a
variety of other recreational pursuits obtained so that the crew
had some diversions. Also, only the best caterers were obtained
to provide the crew with better food than they were accustomed
to having on other location films. In short, the crew was won over
by their belief that everything that could be done was being done

to make a difficult location bearable. The key to maintaining this kind of working relationship with a crew is based on the development of trust. Crew members are human beings and will respond to being treated as such. If they perceive that they are being treated as machines, they will respond accordingly. Delays and other problems will result and the picture and its budget will suffer.

Inevitably, and perhaps constructively, there will be complaints on a picture. At the end of ten weeks, for example, even the most adventurous and expensive caterer will begin serving meals that the crew has had before. Very few crews end up praising the caterers doing their movie. But food is a traditional source for complaints. Given the pressures of production, some amount of complaining or venting frustrations and anger may be helpful. The producer in concert with the production manager should make himself available to hear such complaints whether they are picked up in informal discussions or in a more structured way. Again, the crew is in a position to repay this kind of attention in many ways. From a willingness to work into what otherwise would be meal penalty to a willingness to relax other union requirements, crews do have the opportunity to repay kindnesses or care that has been extended in their direction.

MANAGING CREW MORALE

The development of a proper esprit among the crew is often impeded by the actions of the studio. It is not coincidence that t-shirts and warm-up jackets and the like are frequently given to crew members. The psychology is simple. By giving them a symbol of the production they are working on, some effort toward building a cohesive team is achieved. Money for t-shirts, belt buckles, or jackets is not money that can be seen on the screen. For this reason, these costs are often opposed by tight-fisted studio executives. It is very difficult to convince a studio executive who has not lived through a production on location that these benefits will ultimately save large amounts of money by helping to cut production days. A cooperative and efficient crew can save far more than the comparatively minor cost of jackets or cast parties or the like. It should be remembered that an average production day costs somewhere between $50,000 and $75,000. That amount of money buys a great many t-shirts.

THE PRODUCTION MANAGER'S VIEWPOINT

As a production manager, Michael Rachmil has had the opportunity to work on films where the producer was present and also on films where the producer was absent. He believes that he can function more effectively working in close collaboration with a producer. "I like to get together at the end of the day with the producer to say we've done this, this, and this. The producer can interject his thoughts and a plan of action can be evolved." From Rachmil's standpoint, "A good producer is a producer who really cares about the project, who stays with it and is there in the trenches on location when things go wrong. A good producer cares about all aspects of the movie, knows what his role is, when to step in, and when not to step in, and backs his people when things get tough. He's the man who ultimately goes on the line and says, 'This is what we do.' "

Rachmil prefers the close interaction with a producer who is present to the dealing by telephone with one who is absent. He concludes, "Sometimes circumstances dictate that the producer is the better person to handle a specific problem. When I can work closely with a producer who is himself a presence on a film, I know I can work at my most efficient level."

MANAGING THE BUDGET

Much has been made of problems or troubles that occur during the production of a picture. Nowhere is Murphy's Law—If Something Can Go Wrong, It Will—more constant than in the shooting of a film. Even simple pictures are plagued with minor mishaps that slow down production and threaten the schedule and the budget. This need not be restricted to location pictures. Things as simple as smoke effects not working, or lights burning out, or makeup or hair not being right may interfere with the normal shooting day on a studio picture. In the final analysis, there is no easy picture—each picture is a war. They have differing battlegrounds, but they all have to be fought hard from beginning to end.

CONTINGENCIES AND COMPLETION GUARANTORS

It is very difficult to quantify the risk of the unexpected into a contingency sum that is added on to the budget total. A contingency, in a budget, is an amount of money not allocated to a specific account. It is instead earmarked for a special account to cover any budget overage that may arise. Most completion guarantors will require a contingency account of 10 percent of the entire budget before agreeing to insure any production overages. Thus, a production would have to spend more than 110 percent of its budget before the completion guarantor would pick up the financing burden. On the other hand, if no claim for additional funding is made on the completion guarantor, it will generally refund half of the premium paid (usually around 6 percent of the budget) as a "no-claims bonus."

COST CONTROLS

In terms of cost controls, one of a production's most disheartening events is to see a major film scene left on the cutting room floor after the picture has been through the editing process. This kind of waste should be avoidable in most cases. We confronted just such a situation in the making of *Barbarosa*. Midway through the picture, the writer, director, and I concluded that a costly comedy sequence in which Gary Busey was to ride a bucking cow at a fair didn't really belong in the movie. The wrangler working the show would not guarantee that he could deliver a bucking cow, and we therefore could spend one week shooting a scene that might never work. More importantly, we decided that the burlesque quality of the scene was wrong for the picture and would never survive the picture's final cut. We notified the studio that we wanted to drop the sequence and we were told that this was the studio's favorite scene. I flew to Los Angeles and convinced the studio that they were dealing with a carefully considered position held by the producer, director, and writer. The studio, although not usually presented with requests to drop scenes before they are shot, reluctantly acquiesced. The production was saved $500,000 by facing a problem during production instead of waiting until the editing process. Action of this sort can only be accomplished if egos are submerged in favor of rational management decisions. In the case of *Barbarosa*, we had a production team able to do just that.

A useful tool in monitoring the costs during production is the computer. In earlier years, all costs were reported back to the studio and precise reconciliations took as long as two weeks to get back to the unit on location. It was extremely difficult to keep tabs on all the accounts in a budget when the reporting system was that antiquated. Today, most films have a computer terminal on location. This permits location auditors to enter all costs on a daily basis and compare the projected expenses in each account against the actual costs. In this way, close controls can be maintained and the cost area of a production can be effectively managed from a distant location.

LOCATION CONCERNS

Barbarosa posed other problems typical of location pictures. Weather, for example, plagued us as it has countless pictures before. We had an unusual amount of rainfall, which necessitated the extensive use of cover sets, which are sets available for filming without regard to weather. Careful production management will provide for cover sets wherever there is exterior shooting that could be interrupted by weather. The juggling of these contingencies is an important part of production management. If done correctly, the production unit should have something to shoot every day, regardless of weather.

When a picture is shot in difficult terrain in a remote area, special logistical problems may be presented. Locations must be selected with an eye to travel time as well as the accessibility for trucks and other unit vehicles. Often the creative director has to have his ardor cooled somewhat by the realities of the logistics. It is one thing for the director to bravely hike to some remote location. It is quite something else to move all of the support vehicles into place.

Time is the critical factor in these considerations, because when shooting a picture time is money. The person inexperienced in production always tends to misjudge how long things take to do. A simple move on location, for example, represents a minimum of 1½ hours. It takes 30 minutes to load the trucks, 30 minutes to turn them and move, and 30 minutes to unload them and get set up. Even stage moves in a studio will take approximately 1 hour to accomplish. Many studio officials have no conception of how long it takes to move across the hall on a sound stage to a different set. If they ever came to watch the painstaking progress of moving everything from coffee machines and makeup tables to cables and tools they would see where an hour goes. There are no surprises in this area. There is simply a problem for the unit that doesn't properly account for move time and schedule accordingly. Again, time is money.

Other location problems may be insurable risks. If there is a camera failure or the film stock itself is defective, insurance will pay for reshooting. Likewise, principal cast members and the director are generally insured to protect against their illness or incapacity. The cost of such insurance will exceed $100,000 on a typical film, but the protection afforded is vitally important.

To avoid costly delays occasioned by mistakes on the part of the crew, there is no better instrument than a fully detailed shooting schedule. As prepared during preproduction, this document describes the needs of each scene in the picture. If all of the required props, effects, costumes, hairstyles, makeup, and the like have been approved by the director during preproduction, the possibility of delays will be greatly diminished. No matter how careful the preparation, there are still situations where the success of a shooting day will be in the hands of the director. Some directors adapt brilliantly to the pressure of the unexpected, while others tend to fall apart under the pressure. There is much to be said for a director who can scramble and improvise in order to adjust to the vicissitudes of production.

THE DOMINO EFFECT

A principle not always clearly understood is the domino effect of certain production decisions. Adding more extras to a scene, for example, may affect more than the extras account in the budget. You may have to feed, house, transport, and/or costume them. If they have to be transported it may require another vehicle and another driver. Thus, by the operation of the domino effect, several accounts in the budget would have to be increased by virtue of the decision to add more extras. Many, many production decisions have the domino effect built into them and they should be closely scrutinized to make certain that all the negative effects have been recognized.

REPORTING AIDS—THE CALL SHEET AND THE DAILY PRODUCTION REPORT

Two documents that are used on every film to facilitate the exchange of information are the Call Sheet and the Daily Production Report. The Call Sheet is handed out to each crew member near the close of the shooting day. It provides the specific information pertinent to the next day of shooting. What scenes will be shot, what time is the call to be on the set, what props, makeup, costumes, hairstyles, special effects, and other specifics are shown on this sheet. It is prepared by an assistant director with assistance from the director and the production manager. A copy of the Call Sheet is also posted in the production office so that every member of the cast and crew will know exactly what is planned for each shooting day.

The Daily Production Report is a recap of the progress of the production. It provides a current estimate of where the film stands with respect to production and shooting schedule. The impact of weather and illness are evaluated and a terse, clear presentation of the film's progress is thus available for both the unit and the financing group. This document resolves any confusion as to where a production stands on a daily basis and gives the producer a handy tool for conversations with the director or the studio.

PRODUCTION POLITICS

There are times in the course of production when the producer may find himself mired in a welter of political problems. The producer's influence on a film may be dramatically affected should trouble arise involving the director and the stars. In many instances the combination of work pressure and out-of-control egos will produce serious problems. If these difficulties are present, the studio may be called upon to mediate the dispute. Should this occur, you are well advised to anticipate that the studio will tend to side with the director in any producer-director problem, and with the star in any producer-star difficulty. Both directors and actors figure more importantly than the producer in the production phase of a picture.

The politics of production can run from the creation of an ideal collaboration such as occurred in *Barbarosa* to the very difficult situation where the producer is little more than an employee for hire. In the former instance, the integrity of the film becomes the

_____ DAY OF SHOOTING
SHOOTING CALL_____

CALL SHEET

DATE _____

PICT. _____ NO._____ DIR. _____

SET	SCS.	LOC.
SET	SCS.	LOC.
SET	SCS.	LOC.
SET	SCS.	LOC.
SET	SCS.	LOC.
SET	SCS.	LOC.
SET	SCS.	LOC.
SET	SCS.	LOC.

CAST AND DAY PLAYERS	PART OF	MAKEUP	SET CALL	REMARKS

ATMOSPHERE AND STANDINS		THRU GATE		

ASST. DIR. _____ UNIT PROD. MGR. _____

PRODUCTION REQUIREMENTS

PF 904 REV.

PICTURE _____   DATE _____

	NO.	ITEM	TIME		NO.	ITEM	TIME		NO.	ITEM	TIME
CAMERA		CAMERAMAN		**ELECTRICAL**		GAFFER		**TRANSPORTATION**		CAMERA TRUCK	
		OPERATOR				BEST BOY				INSERT CAR	
		ASSISTANT				LAMP OPERATOR				STANDBY CAR	
		ASSISTANT				LOCAL #40 MAN TO:				SPECIAL EQUIPMENT	
		EXTRA CAMERA				HOOK-UP DR. RMS.					
		EXTRA OPERATOR				OPERATE GENERATOR				BUSSES:	
		EXTRA ASSISTANT				OPERATE WIND MACH.					
						HEAT STAGE					
		KEY GRIP				PORTABLE TELEPHONE				PICTURE CARS & TRUCK	
		2ND GRIP				SIREN/WIG-WAG					
		EXTRA GRIPS				WORK LIGHTS					
		CRANE & CREW				GAS GENERATOR				TRUCKS:	
		CRAB DOLLY									
CONSTRUCTION		CRAFT SERVICE MAN		**MUSIC**		MUSIC REPRESENTATIVE					
		LANDSCAPE MAN				PIANO				SCHOOLROOM TRAILERS	
		PAINTER				PRACTICAL-DUMMY-TUNE				DRESSING RM. TRAILERS	
		PROP. MAKERS				MUSIC TRACKS & CUTTER					
		PLUMBER				P. B.					
		MECH. EFFECTS MEN						**SOUND**		SOUND MIXER	
		WARD. CHECK RM.				SIDELINE ORCHESTRA				SOUND RECORDER	
		BENCHES FOR PEOPLE				SINGERS				BOOM OPERATOR	
		SALAMANDERS								CABLE MAN	
		PROCESS BODY		**PROCESS**		PROCESS CAMERAMAN				EXTRA CABLE MAN	
		PLYWOOD SCHOOLROOM				PROCESS CAMERA				P. A. SYSTEM	
		PLYWOOD DR. RMS.				PROJ. MACH. & CREW				PLAYBACK MACH. & OPER.	
						STEREO MACH. & CREW				ACETATE REC'DER & OPR.	
		PORTABLE DR. RMS.				PLATES:					
MAKEUP		MAKEUP MAN		**PROPERTY**		PROPERTY MAN		**CAFE**		HOT LUNCHES	
		EXTRA MAKEUP MEN				ASST. PROP. MAN				BOX LUNCHES	
		HAIR STYLIST				EXTRA ASST. PROP. MEN				DINNERS	
		EXTRA HAIR STYLISTS				SET DRESSER				GALS. COFFEE	
		BODY MAKEUP WOMAN				DRAPERY MAN				GALS. CHOCOLATE	
						FIXTURE MAN				DOZ. DOUGHNUTS	
POLICE		DOORMAN				WARDROBE RACKS				SCRIPT SUPERVISOR	
		WARDROBE CHECKER				MAKEUP TABLES				EXTRA ASST. DIR.	
		WATCHMEN:				BIRDS, ETC.:				STILLMAN	
		NIGHT DAY				WAGONS, ETC.:		**MISCELLANEOUS**		REGISTERED NURSE	
		LOCKER RM. ATTENDANTS:									
		MAN MATRON								MOVIOLA MACHINE	
		STUDIO POLICE				HUMANE REPRESENTATIVE				PROJECTIONIST	
		MOTORCYCLE POLICE				WRANGLERS				FILM:	
		POLICE PERMITS				LIVESTOCK:					
										FURN. FOR DRESSING RM.	
WARDROBE		COSTUMER (MEN)								FURN. FOR SCHOOL	
		COSTUMER (WOMEN)				DEPT. REPRESENTATIVE				FURN. FOR OFFICE	
		EXTRA COSTUMER (MEN)		**PHOTO EFFECTS**							
		EXTRA COSTUMER (WOMEN)				CAMERA		**FIRE**		FIREMAN	
										FIRE WARDEN	

DEPARTMENT _____   SPECIAL INSTRUCTIONS _____

_____
_____
_____
_____
_____

ASST. DIR. _____   UNIT PROD. MGR. _____

DAILY PRODUCTION REPORT

	1st Unit	2nd Unit	Ren.	Test	Travel	Holidays	Change-Over	Retakes & Add. Scns.	Total	SCHEDULE	
										AHEAD	
No. Days Scheduled								✕			
No. Days Actual								✕		BEHIND	

Title _____ Date _____

Producer _____ Prod. # _____

Date Started _____ Director _____

Scheduled Finish Date _____ Est. Finish Date _____

Sets _____

_____ Location _____

Crew Call _____ Shooting Call _____ First Shot _____ Lunch _____ Till _____

Company Dismissed: At Studio _____ On Location _____ Dinner _____ Till _____ Last Shot _____

At Headquarters _____

SCRIPT SCENES AND PAGES

	SCENES	PAGES
Script		
Taken Prev.		
Taken Today		
Total to Date		
To be Taken		

MINUTES

	Scene No.	Added Scenes	Retakes
Prev.			
Today			
Total			

SET-UPS

Prev.	
Today	
Total	

ADDED SCENES

Prev.	
Today	
Total	

RETAKES

	PAGES	SCENES

FILM USE	GROSS	PRINT	NO GOOD	WASTE
Prev.				
Today				
To Date				

Sound Tracks _____

1/4" ROLLS _____

FILM INVENTORY

Starting Inventory	
Additional Received	
Total	

CAST — WEEKLY AND DAY PLAYERS

Worked—W   Finished—F   Rehearsal—R   Test—T
Started—S   Hold—H   Travel—TR

CAST	CHARACTER	W H S F R T	Makeup Wdbe.	TR

WORK TIME

Report on Set	Dismiss on Set

MEALS

Out	In

TRAVEL TIME

Leave for Location	Arrive on Location	Leave Location	Arrive at Hdq.

EXTRA TALENT									
No.	Rate	1st Call	Set Dismiss	Final Dismiss	Adj.	MPV	No.	Rate	1st Call

Assistant Director _____ Production Manager _____

STAFF AND CREW

Production Manager
1st Asst. Director
1st Asst. Director
2nd Asst. Director
2nd Asst. Director
Trainee
Script Supervisor

Cameraman
Camera Operator
Camera Operator
Asst. Cameraman
Asst. Cameraman
Asst. Cameraman

Key Grip
2nd Grip
Crane Grip
Extra Grips
First Aid
Craft Service Man
Greens Man
Painter
Propmaker
Plumber
Special Effects Man

Makeup Artist
Makeup Artist
Hair Stylist
Hair Stylist
Body Makeup
Doormen
Watchmen

STAFF AND CREW

Set Decorator
Property Master
Asst. Propmaster
Asst. Propmaster

Fixture Man
Swing Gang Man

Wranglers
Wranglers (Local)

Mixer
Recorder
Boom Operator
Cable Man
Playback

Driver Captain
Drivers
Drivers (Local)
Location Auditor
Timekeeper
Publicity Man
Art Director
Stillman
Dialogue Coach
Technical Advisor
Stunt Coordinator
Welfare Worker
Projectionist
Film Editor
Asst. Editor
Sync. Men
Rehearsal Pianist

EQUIPMENT

Cars
Bus
Stretchout
Camera Truck
Grip Truck/trlr.
Electric Truck/trlr.
Generator Truck/trlr.
Prop Truck/trlr.
Wardrobe Truck/trlr.
Sound Truck/trlr.
Set Dressing Truck/trlr.
Special Effects Truck/trlr.
Utility Truck
Pickup Truck
Picture Cars
Insert Car
Crane
Horse Truck
Water Wagon
Honey Wagon/ Dr. Rms.
Dr. Room trlr.
Portable Dr. Room
School Room
Horses
Horses (Local)
Animals

Policemen

Fireman

Coordinator

Men's Wardrobe

Women's Wardrobe

Gaffer

Best Boy

Lamp Operators

Local #40 Man

Generator Operator

Local IA

SPECIAL STAFF AND CREW

MEALS SERVED

SPECIAL EQUIPMENT AND LIVESTOCK

COMMENTS — DELAYS (EXPLANATION) — CAST, STAFF, AND CREW ABSENCE

PF 907 B

deciding factor in any dispute. What is best for the movie is the right answer to any question that comes up. In the latter model, control may rest with the most powerful element, without regard to any other consideration. There may be ways to extricate yourself from this quandary, but there will also be times when nothing can be done.

In summation, the producer during the time of production should fulfill his responsibility as the principal arbiter of monetary decisions. No matter how such problems are couched, they inevitably become a problem of money on the one side versus creativity on the other. Unfortunately, the lines separating the two competing interests are usually murky to say the least. Requests for further equipment will always be supported by the theory that the cost of the equipment will be more than covered by the saving in shooting time. These are balance questions which warrant discussion with the production manager, the director, and any other interested party. The effective producer, however, will hear both sides and will work to arrive at effective compromises wherever possible.

It has been suggested that Hollywood is entering an era of belt tightening and greater insistence on the supervision of its product. The jury remains out on the effect of this movement on the producing community.

The word "producer" covers a multitude of functions and roles. The description of the producer as an active force during production need not connote that only individuals involved in production should consider themselves effective producers. An examination of the working producers of today discloses the existence of specialists in development, fund raising, line production, and marketing. Each producer will define his activities in a somewhat different fashion. For any producer concerned with the financial and creative directions of his film, however, it is suggested that the only place to be during production is where the movie is being filmed.

8

Collaboration with the Director

In the halycon days of the motion picture business, the producer was the critical element in getting movies made. When the David Selznicks and Samuel Goldwyns ruled the roost, a producer enjoyed a degree of prominence that he rarely experiences today. He was the unquestioned hub of all creative and financial matters having to do with the film he was producing. Over the years, fashions in filmmaking have changed. Producers have surrendered a great deal of their creative leadership in filmmaking to the director, and have expanded, to a degree, their control over the financial and entrepreneurial aspects of movie-making. In the recent past, the medium seemed to belong almost exclusively to the director. The director was considered the "auteur" of the film and financing institutions rushed to extend to him complete control over all aspects of filmmaking. The pendulum has swung back today and the producer enjoys something of a resurgence from the standpoint of influence and day-to-day control of the filmmaking process. In part this is a result of the comparatively unsuccessful track record of films made during the "auteur" period. It may also be traced to the new emphasis being placed on financial controls over production.

The producer has not achieved parity with the director in the eyes of the studios, however. As a general rule he is paid far less than an equally experienced director. He is not deemed to be an element of sufficient stature to cause a studio to green light a picture. An acceptable director must be secured before a studio will slate a film for production. In earlier years, this system operated in reverse. The producer made the picture happen. This may be illustrated by the fact that in 1939 the same director made both *The Wizard of Oz* and *Gone With the Wind,* and very few moviegoers can recall his name.

SELECTION OF A DIRECTOR

As a producer, then, one of your foremost tasks is to try to secure the services of a director acceptable to you and to your financiers. A handful of directors are considered "bankable," or of such stature that any company would be overjoyed to have them work on its film. Names like Steven Spielberg, Sydney Pollack, or George Lucas would certainly find their way onto any such list. Other names, particularly directors with recent hit pictures, might receive qualified support from most quarters. Still, while such choices may please the financial types, they may be very wrong creatively. Not every talented director can direct every kind of film, whether it be a comedy, an action-adventure piece, or a science fiction thriller. There are several guidelines that you may employ to assist you in choosing the right director.

Talent is a subjective commodity. Ultimately, you must decide for yourself whether a director does or does not possess it. In your evaluation of a film, the "look," the performances, the handling of the telling of the story, and the overall combination of all the elements that make up the film must be assessed. How they relate to your project must also be considered. It is as useless to typecast directors as it is to typecast actors. Simply because a director crafted a successful horror film is not reason enough to believe that he cannot direct light comedy. The best insight you can get before making your decision is to sit with the director and hear his views on your material. In most cases, it will be his vision that finally finds its way to the screen.

There may be a problem for the new producer in getting a director to consider his material. Hot directors are deluged with scripts by studios and independent producers. They are also protected from random submissions by their agents and lawyers. It is through these watchdogs, however, that producers are able to get material to a director. Depending on how hot the director may be, this task could be as difficult as getting the movie made. Persistence and a belief in the material are the two most important qualities a producer can employ in trying to bring the right director to the project. Perhaps a grain of common sense is equally worthwhile. It is, after all, very unlikely that Steven Spielberg will choose to direct your film. The more realistic the producer is in trying to secure a director, the more likely it is that he will be successful.

If you are convinced that a certain director is the best person for the job, you should endeavor to extract a commitment from him. This is, of course, subject to his availability, his compensation, and your being able to find some group willing to finance the film. Hopefully, all of this will come together in a timely fashion. If it does, it will be the beginning of a collaboration that spans the duration of the film, from preproduction to marketing.

COLLABORATION IN PREPRODUCTION

As preproduction gets under way, the producer and director should work to develop a healthy atmosphere that will facilitate an effective collaboration. Inevitably there will be overlapping responsibilities and areas of shared interests. First, both individuals should share a total concern with the evolution of the shooting script, focusing not only on the story and the dialogue but also upon issues such as production problems and budgetary constraints. As you and the director approach this task from different perspectives, the result of a good collaboration can only enhance the overall progress of the film.

CASTING AND CREWING

When selecting the crew, it is advisable to work with the director and the production manager to pool all available information about work records and salary levels. If questions arise, calls to previous employers may resolve any lingering doubts about a crew member's skills or competence. Although the crew members will be ultimately responsible to the director in the shooting of the movie, it is essential that the hiring process be opened up to include both the production manager and the producer. This is the only way to tap into all information sources and to avoid, wherever possible, costly problems down the road.

As for casting, the twin issues of correctness for the part and compensation must be resolved. Often, the producer and director will choose to work out an elaborate routine of "good cop/bad cop." Both will play out assigned roles in trying to convince an actor to accept a part or in convincing his agent to accept a deal at terms most advantageous to the production. Actors' deals are sufficiently complex today and their representation so adroit and so skilled that these ploys are more in the way of self-defense than exploitation. Typically, the producer will be the bad cop in this arrangement. At other times, the roles may be reversed.

In 1973, I produced a film entitled *Westworld*, which was written and directed by Michael Crichton. Crichton was most skilled at this game-playing aspect of the casting process. He saw it as a necessary instrument in accomplishing the desired end. As he puts it, "The producer can say, 'There's nothing I can do about it. I have this unreasonable, temperamental director,' and use that as an excuse to get things done. The director can say, 'What can I do? The producer's got his hands on the money and I really can't help you with this.' That's a kind of accepted lie that keeps the wheels turning."

OTHER PREPRODUCTION RESPONSIBILITIES

There are many other areas where the producer and the director can function together during preproduction. Many producers enjoy doing groundwork such as preliminary location scouting and presenting those options to the director. This may prove very time-efficient for the director as it frees him for other pursuits. Crichton describes a similar collaboration with producer John Foreman in the preparation of the film *The Great Train Robbery*. "We had a large scene with lots of horses and coaches. Whatever it is in me, horses make me exhausted and bored. I have no feeling for horses except to get them out of the way as soon as possible. Foreman likes horses. Our horses and antique coach problems were compelling for him. He just took it over and arranged it all. It was very time-consuming, and I was most appreciative." Many directors are extremely eager to share such preproduction chores with their producers. They are presented with viable production options without the necessity of doing the preliminary work themselves.

BUDGET

One area that is fraught with possible conflict is the preparation of the board and budget. This issue highlights one of the real anomalies of the picture business. In other businesses, the more experienced the worker, the more cost-efficient and the less wasteful he becomes. Movies have always been an exception to that rule. In films, it is only the first-time director who is given a limited budget and a short shooting schedule to work with. The experienced director demands a longer schedule with higher paid craftsmen and more frills at every turn. Thus, the veteran director will deliver his film for a far greater cost than the new director would deliver a comparable project. As this is a fact of life in the picture business, the producer has little choice but to work within this format and endeavor to hold costs down wherever he can. The seeds of any discord in this area are sown in the preproduction period when the budget and board are evolved. In this give and take process, the producer is advised to do the best he can, consistent with his perception of the baseline needs of the film.

PRODUCTION

A few years ago, the prevailing notion of the producer's role during production was to keep the studio off the director's back, and to permit the director to make his film. Today, it is more a matter of establishing some basis where the producer and director can both perform tasks that are necessary to the film's progress. On a basic level, the producer can be where the director is not. He can supervise construction, work in the production office with the production manager, deal with the studio by telephone, handle the press, and perform many other functions while the director is on the floor filming. The splitting up of these chores enables the production to move forward at its most effective level.

On a day-to-day basis, the producer can supply the director with a commodity that is often in very short supply—objectivity. Again, Michael Crichton: "If you get to a decision that has to do with the overall picture, the only person the director has to speak with is the producer. If the director turns to the cameraman about whether a shot should be day or night, the cameraman will think of the nicest-looking shot. If he turns to an actor, the actor will think about whether it's a good scene for him. The only person besides the director who thinks about the picture as a whole is the producer."

DAILIES

The most immediate need for objectivity in production arises from each day's viewing of dailies. The picture now begins to take a finite shape on the screen. Scenes will either "work" or "not work." The director should welcome the producer's point of view on performances and technical matters as it will provide a unique overview that may not be otherwise available. As it would be in any discourse on a sensitive subject, discretion is a necessary part of these communications. Thus, a producer will generally do better discussing problems he has with dailies when the director is alone and not surrounded by other members of the cast or crew. If handled properly, there is no reason to cause any anxiety on the part of the director.

CAST ANXIETIES

Often, producer and director work in tandem to allay any anxieties the actors may have. This is not so much in relation to their parts, where the director should shore up any insecurities they may have, but rather in connection with their overall relationship to the movie. Temperament problems abound on movie sets and they end up costing huge amounts of money. Nothing is more comforting to an actor than the belief that his needs, real or imagined, are being addressed.

On my first studio picture, *Westworld,* the cast was headed by Yul Brynner. Brynner required a fitting for special contact lenses for the picture. The fitting was to take place in the San Fernando Valley, some ten miles from his Beverly Hills hotel. He requested a limousine for the drive and I had to inform him that the film's low budget made such luxuries impossible. Brynner's response was curt and direct, "Fine," he said, "I won't be wearing lenses in the picture." Trying to rescue a failing situation, I asked him if my secretary could drive him. He readily agreed and, in her aging Mustang, she drove him to the Valley for his fitting. As long as he felt taken care of, he, like most actors, was happy.

STUDIO POLITICS

While not the only task of the producer, the job of coping with the demands of the studio or other financing group during production is a very important one. Crichton neatly characterizes the nature of this problem: "I think about films as an anxiety cascade where everybody in a higher position mops up the anxiety of the people below. The director's job is, in part, to soak up the anxiety of the actors. Similarly, if the studio develops anxiety, it's the producer's job to step in and hold their hands, to say the money is safe and the picture's going to be okay. That's what the studio wants to hear.

"A director may be resentful if producers don't control the studio and keep them off his back. If a studio gets overanxious, a director can never really calm the waters because he is not in the end the money person."

POSTPRODUCTION

During postproduction the director spends most of his time in the editing room with the editor and the editorial assistants. Some directors welcome a close collaboration with the producer during this time, but most do not. As Crichton says, "The producer should wait as long as he can stand it to see a cut of the picture. Then, having given his comments, he should again wait as long as possible before seeing it again. If he sees it once a week, or as often as the director sees it, very soon he will be as lacking in objectivity as the director."

There is much to be done in the management of postproduction budget and the meeting of deadlines to occupy the producer's time. That is producer work. As far as the collaboration goes, again the key word is *objectivity*. The more of it the producer can maintain, and the more articulate he is in explaining his position, the better the end product on the screen is likely to be.

DISAGREEMENTS

Some disagreements will inevitably occur. By most accounts, any struggle should be resolved on the basis of how strongly the producer or the director feels about the question at issue. As with any healthy relationship, it usually makes better sense to go along with the stronger conviction, whether it be that of the producer or the director. In the event both have strong points of view, it may make sense to try it both ways or otherwise accommodate both points of view for as long as possible. If no satisfaction can be obtained through this process, then things will have to work out the best they can. It bears repeating to again mention the problem of publicly airing a disagreement between producer and director. Crichton continues to view this problem in terms of the inherent anxiety present. "You have to expect that in large cooperative ventures involving a great deal of money, like movies, anxiety is rife. There's lots and lots of it, and it's never to the advantage of anyone to heighten the anxiety. Disagreements let the studio, which is inevitably nervous, become more nervous. The studio will react saying, 'My God, the director and the producer don't get along.' At that point, everybody's job becomes harder."

RELATIONSHIPS

In characterizing the collaboration between producer and director, some recognition must be made of the fact that there will be varying strengths and weaknesses in both individuals extending to both their personalities and also to the respective power or muscle they bring to the partnership. A very powerful producer such as Ray Stark exerts so much influence and sway with the financiers that he becomes, in effect, a miniature studio unto himself. A director who works with him is sheltered from many of the pressures normally exerted by studios. In lieu of studio pressure, however, the director will have to hold his own in dealing with the producer. In the end, the collaboration between producer and director will be shaped by the personalities and preferences of both. There is a finite body of work to be done, but a wide range of options available for completing it. A producer with sufficient competence at his craft should be an active participant not only in these choices but also in the determination of the final shape of the film as well.

CREDIT AND BLAME

If the film fails commercially, where is the blame accorded? Rarely in today's Hollywood is the producer held accountable for a commercial failure. If the film is successful, his career will proceed upward. Studios may compete to try to secure his next project. His fees and profit participations will likewise be increased. In general, the "successful" producer will be thought of as "hot" in a community that places great importance on heat.

As for the director, Crichton explains, "If a movie gets spectacular reviews but doesn't do business, the director is off the hook. If a picture gets hideous reviews and does a lot of business, everybody is content. A picture that gets bad reviews and does no business is probably going to be laid at the feet of the director. That's the style of the times."

At the heart of the collaboration between producer and director is the fact that each sits atop a power base which is at the center of picture-making. The director commands the creative direction of a film. He is ultimately responsible for the film's creative content. The producer, on the other hand, is directly responsible for the financial framework of the picture. These polarities, of course, overlap. It is in their interaction, in the inevitable tension between creativity and money, that the basis of a collaboration exists.

9

Postproduction

It's not unusual in the production of a film to hear someone say, "We'll fix it in postproduction." Postproduction is of little interest to the lay person because it lacks much of the glamour of production. However, to the knowledgeable, it is as critical a phase of a movie's evolution as is production. Postproduction is anything but a collection of mechanical steps. It is a creative process populated by highly creative artists who more often than not enhance the films they work on, and only too often rescue the director from impossible situations he has gotten himself into.

THE FUNCTIONS OF POSTPRODUCTION

The creation in movies of moods that the audience understandably takes for granted is primarily a function of postproduction. The classic movie genres, from comedies to musicals, from suspense thrillers to epics, all owe much of their success to the contribution of the editor and the rest of the postproduction team. Special effects, opticals, music, and sound effects all have important roles to play in this process. There are occasions when a good sound effect or music cue is one that is so innocuous as to be unnoticeable. There are many other times, however, when the sound effect or the music cue carries the scene and leads the audience into the frame of mind that the performances were originally supposed to create.

Reflect, for example, on the number of times you have discovered yourself moved more by the music behind a certain movie scene than by the action itself. If movies are the manipulation of reality, as one director has suggested, then the tools of postproduction are pivotal in effecting this end.

THE POSTPRODUCTION BUDGET

If there is a general rule about postproduction, it is that it takes longer than scheduled and costs more than the budget allows. In part this results from an inadequate understanding of the steps involved and a willingness on the part of producers to leave these supposedly mechanical processes to the technicians who they presume will carry them out. This is not only bad management, it is also bad judgment. Postproduction can add much to your film and can often be the difference between a film's working and not working, commercially and creatively.

Jim Potter is an editor with vast postproduction experience. He serves as vice president of postproduction for Tri-Star Pictures, capping twenty-five years with major companies and independents. He feels that postproduction budgets will inexorably creep upward because the percentage in dollars versus the total cost of the film is comparatively small. "Whereas the production unit supports 100 to 125 people on a daily basis with costs up to $125,000 a day, postproduction has but three or four people on a regular basis with perhaps as many as another twelve on a part-time basis." It is also very common to trim monies from the postproduction budget when you are trying to get the budget approved for production. The theory is that you can put it back later when the studio is delighted with what they have seen in dailies or in the rough cut. Adds Potter, "It is even worse than that. In production you can steal from the paint account to provide funds for wardrobe, or steal from wardrobe to help out in set dressing. Postproduction is the end of the line. There are no other accounts to steal from."

Major studio postproduction budgets have gradually risen with guild increases and inflation until they now routinely exceed $1 million. One of the major reasons for this is the change in the salary of the film editor. A short time ago, the editor was viewed as a technician rather than an artist. Now he is looked upon as a creative force who can truly help shape a film and he is compensated by a multiple of five to ten times what he used to make. That salary alone has greatly changed the postproduction budget.

In addition, the cost of sound has risen dramatically as mixing room time is extended by zealous directors. At an approximate cost of $30,000 a week, delays in the mixing room can wreak havoc with the postproduction budget.

THE POSTPRODUCTION SCHEDULE: TIME VERSUS MONEY

The amount of time postproduction takes is a much debated topic. Schedules for postproduction usually run about twenty-eight to thirty-two weeks. In practice, forty- to forty-two-week periods are anything but uncommon. Need it take that long? Probably not. Although there would be inevitable losses in quality, it is certainly possible to complete all postproduction duties in about sixteen weeks. This would assume the editor's assembling the picture as it was being shot, allow four weeks for the director to do his cut, four weeks for music and effects, and four weeks for dubbing and printing. This is very close to the schedule followed by low-budget films and very far from the typical studio picture.

Even the most cost-conscious postproduction supervisors are aware that adding personnel to speed along a film's progress may have a deleterious effect on the film's quality. More people may shorten the schedule, but it may also alter the rhythms and cadences of the picture. This may never get to an audience's conscious mind, but such shifts in a movie's internal rhythm will certainly work against an audience's enjoyment of a picture. This fact creates a natural reluctance to merely add bodies to achieve time savings. Some people *do* do it and discount any editorial variations in the end result. In the final analysis, it is important to keep some pressure on the postproduction group to finish the film with all deliberate speed. But if you squeeze too hard you will almost certainly do a disservice to the picture.

THE POSTPRODUCTION PROCESS

The postproduction process doesn't start at the end of principal photography. Rather, it begins with the processing of film and transferring of sound at the end of the first day's shooting. This film and sound track will be subject to a quality control review and will go immediately into the editorial process. At this stage the postproduction team is entirely composed of members of the editorial staff—the editor, his assistant(s) and apprentice(s). Opticals and special effects may be at work at this time, but they can be considered separately.

THE FILM EDITOR

In the initial stages of postproduction, the laboring oar is carried by the film editor. The editor is hired by the director and the producer, usually with the approval of the studio. Editors tend to develop reputations for proficiency in a certain genre such as comedy or action-adventure. Or certain editors may always be hired by the same directors if the director finds a special personal or professional compatibility. Some editors, such as Dede Allen or the late Verna Fields, have been so knowledgeable about film as to be major figures in the creative direction and final look of the movie. The editor, in the main, serves at the pleasure of the director. He must therefore focus his energies on carrying out the vision held by the director. In a healthy collaboration, the director and the editor work closely, trying different approaches and experimenting with different nuances. Fundamental shifts in character shadings and even plot will come in the editing of the film. Sometimes these changes are envisioned by the director as the picture is being shot. Often they are simply outgrowths of the many hours spent working on an editing machine trying different approaches. The pacing and the rhythm, both so vitally important to an audience's acceptance of a film, are established during this time.

DAILIES

As the film is being shot, each day's work is shown to the production unit the following day as "dailies." The director, cinematographer, and the various department heads are able to examine critically the makeup of each scene from wardrobe to performance. Dailies are the first barometer of how successfully a film is progressing in the course of production. Some directors will allow the actors the chance to view dailies, while others believe it is not a good idea. Both attitudes are common.

As a film is shot, each scene is covered by the director. Generally, the director will first shoot a "master" shot which will be a wide-angle or a long shot that includes all the characters and all the action. He will then do additional "coverage" to isolate in closeups or medium shots all the elements that make up that sequence. He will finish off with "inserts," which are extreme closeups of specific items such as telephones or cigarettes. Most of these shots will be taken a number of times by the director, each shot being termed a separate take. Only some of the takes will be printed and shown in dailies.

THE EDITING ROOM

Editing rooms are extremely well organized in order to deal efficiently with what may be 1 million feet of printed film. All the film is catalogued and boxed on racks by the apprentice or assistant editor. As the editorial work proceeds, certain takes are chosen and other takes of the same scene are labeled "out-takes" and stored. The entire take is rarely used, however, as other angles are cut in by the editor. The unused portion, or "trim," is also stored so that it can be easily retrieved at a later date. This process is one of constant experimentation as different ideas are tried out and then accepted or rejected.

Some editors today prefer transferring all the film to videotape during the editing process. This makes footage very easy to retrieve and generally simplifies the problems inherent in assembling a picture.

EDITOR'S CUT

After the movie has finished shooting, the editor, either working with the director or on his own, will complete the first assemblage, or editor's cut. Depending on the working relationship between director and editor, this cut could be within a half hour of the final length, or as much as two to three times the final running time. The director will be looking for certain rhythms and timing, and if the lines of communication between the editor and the director are good, the director will begin to get what he wants in this assemblage.

DIRECTOR'S CUT

Guild agreements and industry practice tend to leave the director alone with the picture until he has finished his first cut. Thus, there will be no studio interference or other input at this stage. He will have six weeks to work undisturbed on his cut. If it is a studio picture, there will be studio involvement in the selection of the laboratory, the sound transfer facility, the optical house, and other facilities of this kind.

When the director refines the editor's assemblage into his "director's cut," we have what is customarily referred to as a "rough cut." This is a stage of a movie without music or sound effects, perhaps with missing scenes, many unintelligible or otherwise bad lines of dialogue, and serious mismatches in color, background sound, and other aspects of production.

Although industry professionals claim to be able to view a rough cut as if it were finished film, you are urged to take this claim with a huge grain of salt. Many a producer has learned to his detriment that distributors and exhibitors have sadly overestimated their ability to see and understand a rough cut of a motion picture. A temporary mix to add suggestions of music and sound effects is suggested as a way to bridge the gap for people who are not experienced in seeing "unfinished" films.

If you are producing a studio picture, the production executives will certainly get involved at the rough cut stage. They will have points of view on structure, character, length, and all other components that make up a film. This association can result in a healthy collaboration with the creative elements or a decidedly antagonistic one.

CREATIVE DISAGREEMENTS

As a producer, when faced with differences of opinion at this juncture, it is important to keep any arguments among the creative elements separate from discussions with the studio or other financial source. Such differing viewpoints are quite natural and are common to most films. If studio executives are confronted with disparate opinions, they will have little choice but to intercede and arbitrate between the opposing parties. This could well give rise to decisions that are less in the best interests of the movie, and more in the interests of the politics of the moment. To avoid this result, you should use your good offices to settle any creative arguments within the confines of the creative group. The movie's best interests will then be served.

Previews are also a time-honored way to resolve creative disputes. The picture can be previewed in two different versions and different audience responses can be measured. This happens many times when more than one ending is being tried. These previews should take place before the final mix, if possible, so as to hold costs down.

MUSIC AND SOUND EFFECTS

Once the rough cut changes have been made and the film is in an acceptable version, the next phase of postproduction begins. The postproduction team is expanded to include music and sound effects personnel. The composer and the music editor are hired and shown the film to elicit their feelings. This leads to a session where the director, the editor, and the composer view the film on an editing machine and "spot" where they feel the musical cues belong. The emotional feeling behind these cues is discussed before the composer goes off to do his work. The music editor will work closely with the composer to evolve exact timings for every cue in the picture. This enables the composer to do his work very precisely and ensures that the music will fit exactly as intended. The sound effects people are likewise shown the film so that they can begin to enhance the sound that has been previously recorded. They will now build additional sound material which will augment and enliven the sound portions of the finished film.

LOOPING

Before the film can be mixed, some original dialogue will have to be replaced or rerecorded. This process is called "looping" after the early method of taking the unsatisfactory line and fashioning it into a loop for replaying on a machine. The actor would hear the line over and over in his earphones and would try to synchronize a new reading of the faulty dialogue. Today films use Automated Dialogue Replacement or ADR to accomplish the same end. The dialogue is kept in the same position as it appears in the film and the actor watches it over and over, synchronizing his reading to the picture on the screen. When the director is satisfied, the recording is made then and there. Off-stage voices can be added at the same time to enhance a given scene.

So effective is the ADR process that many an actor's performance can be significantly improved. Willie Nelson, for example, greatly enhanced his performance in *Barbarosa* when he came to the ADR sessions. Perhaps it was simply that he had a second chance at the lines; perhaps he was freer and more willing to experiment without the pressure of holding up a crew of 125 people. Whatever the reason, the important thing to remember is that looping provides a second bite at the apple, a chance to significantly improve performance while at the same time correcting technical problems in the initial recording.

MUSIC SESSIONS

As the composer readies himself for the recording dates, he will use the services of an arranger and copyist to prepare finished sheet music for the recording session. A recording session for a film is not unlike a recording session for a record. The only difference is the addition of a large motion picture screen and a print which has been carefully marked with visual starts and stops for every cue. The conductor, frequently the composer, can see the marks on the print and conduct the orchestra at the same time.

The music budget on feature films is very often exceeded during the course of postproduction. It may be hard to justify this overage since sessions usually finish on time and thus incur no overtime charges. Most often this results from using more musicians than the budget contemplated. Large orchestral sounds emanate from large orchestras. Typically, music sessions begin with a full complement of musicians and gradually dismiss more and more players until they are down to the cues requiring but a handful of musicians. As a cost-conscious producer, once these sessions are scheduled, there is not much you can do except sit back and enjoy one of the exciting times in a picture's evolution.

It is at the planning stages when the fee for the composer is negotiated and when the size of the orchestra is discussed that you can have a real impact on the problem.

SOUND EFFECTS

Like anything else, the best choices in postproduction are often the most expensive and time-consuming. Sound effects are a good example. Some sound effects units can be taken from any stock library without a noticeable effect upon the picture. Others should be custom built for your movie to get exactly the right quality. This includes the many effects that are "foleyed," or created and recorded to fit a particular moment in a film. Named after Jack Foley who created the system some time ago, the foley process lets a team of sound effects specialists recreate the myriad of everyday sounds from clothes rustling to the sound of footsteps on a variety of different surfaces. These sounds are all built on separate units and delivered that way to the mix. Any given reel of motion picture film will have five, ten, or even twenty reels of sound effects running in sequence to achieve the overlapping sounds that are required by the specific scene.

THE DUB OR MIX

The "mix," or "dub," is the blending of the disparate sound elements—dialogue, music, and sound effects—into one cohesive unit. This will involve the balancing of the dialogue tracks with the many effects tracks and the two to four music tracks (each of them carrying three separate channels). Says Potter, "I don't know how to explain the hours of thinking and study that go into this work or the brilliance of some of the people who handle this aspect of postproduction. These craftsmen may dream up off-stage scenes that weren't in the original script or the director's mind that cause a picture to come alive for an audience. This is anything but a mechanical exercise."

Generally, the mix is preceded by a premix, which is a kind of technical rehearsal. The dialogue tracks are evened out and any other problems isolated and dealt with during the week of premixing.

The mixing stage where all of this takes place is essentially a small theatre with a large panel at the rear where the sound editors and mixing editors sit. All the sound elements are pumped through this panel where they can be filtered or otherwise electronically affected to get the desired quality, timbre of sound, and volume. This is a trial and error process and rehearsals provide opportunities to experiment with different approaches. The modern mixing theatre has a wealth of electronic gadgetry which permits the suppression of unwanted background noise as well as the creation of new voice effects such as echos or the sound of people speaking on a telephone. Many are also now equipped with computers to speed up making small changes.

It is difficult to contemplate mixing more than one reel a day. A reel is 1,000 feet or approximately 11 minutes of screen time. Actually, reels today do not hold the full 1,000 feet that they were originally designed to do. This stems from the fact that present-day reels were designed for black and white film. Color film is thicker than its black and white counterpart and takes up more room on the reels, producing a count of somewhat less than 1,000 feet.

The director has the final vote at most mixes, just as he had during principal photography. He can now see the film with all the various elements together and assess how the picture plays. He is able to alter certain nuances in order to achieve the effects he has been striving to attain. Usually he will allow the mixers the opportunity to try different alternatives before making a decision. A good team of mixers will set the creative parameters for a director and enable him to push the limits of the sound capabilities of his picture.

All work in a mixing theatre is done on black and white work prints. When the final mix has been recorded for each reel, the projectionist switches to color for the last runthrough before moving to the next reel. These are some of the most exciting moments in the making of a movie. Having watched hours of experimentation with the dirty black and white work print, it is both exhilarating and rewarding to see the movie unfold in glorious color, complete with a newly mixed sound track.

TECHNOLOGICAL ADVANCEMENTS

Sometimes, according to Potter, an advance in technology will have an inadvertant effect on the speed with which postproduction progresses. Such an advance was the flat bed editing machine. Its large viewing screen provided a major improvement over the traditional moviola editing machine. But, as Potter points out, "It provides the means for multiple pairs of eyes to look at the screen simultaneously. When you've got multiple pairs of eyes, you've got multiple points of view." Still, Jim Potter is a firm advocate of this advance in the editing process. "The time increases pale in importance next to considerations of the overall investment," he concludes.

Many filmmakers wage life and death struggles to get Dolby sound or 70mm for their release prints. Studios tend to resist these efforts for all but the most important or largest-scale films. In the latter case, marketing executives or even exhibitors will pressure for 70mm or Dolby. There are no definitive studies as to whether the addition of Dolby or stereo or 70mm helps sell tickets at the box office. Jim Potter has an interesting point of view in this regard: "I feel that 70mm and 6 track stereo may actually increase box office returns. The contribution that Dolby has made in noise reduction has been very significant. It really works. Yet this is only the beginning of the story. As a filmmaker, you now may find yourself with a Ferrari and no road to run it on. Theatre owners tend not to maintain their equipment because such costs come directly out of their own pockets. In most cases, for example, a 2 track Dolby print will play worse than normal monaural sound. With these kinds of headaches, it is doubtful if the expenses of going to stereo, Dolby, and 70mm will pay off at the other end."

The incremental cost of adding stereo to the mix will usually run as much as $100,000. Such hidden costs as the need to remix in monaural to accommodate television, the need to remix without dialogue for foreign monaural versions, the requirement that the editors, music, and effects personnel be carried throughout the extended mixing period, plus nonbudgeted purchases from stock to optical transfers all have to be added in. In the aggregate, it can be very expensive.

On the other side of the argument is the thinking that the target audience has enormous visual and audio sophistication and will appreciate state of the art sound and picture. It is hard to separate the merits of this argument from what seem to be the ego demands of the filmmakers of today. Perhaps it is best to say that each situation should be considered on its own and all the arguments pro and con weighed carefully each time they are presented.

OPTICALS AND SPECIAL EFFECTS

Before any release printing can be done, all the opticals and special effects, including the film's titles, have to be cut in. Special creative resources will be used to design and shoot the title sequences and to execute the optical effects that are desired for the film. This can be very much of a trial and error process as the optical houses try to create the effects that the director has described to them.

Such films as *Star Wars* have brought special effects to a rarified degree of sophistication. As the creators of these effects and the audiences for whom they are designed become more and more demanding, we can expect greater drains upon picture budgets and the possibility of significant delays in postproduction. Other than an awareness of these phenomena, there is little the producer can do to materially change matters.

THE COMPOSITE PRINT

While the mix is in progress, the negative of the film is being cut by a skilled technician known as a negative cutter. During this process, the negative, untouched since the film was first developed, is meticulously cut to conform to the approved work print. That 35mm strip of picture is then combined with the optical track that results from the mix, and they are printed together to produce an end result called a "composite print." Since the film was shot at different times under very different lighting conditions, sometimes using different film stocks, there remains the problem of balancing the light and color values of the picture. Working with a timer, the director and/or the cinematographer will carefully analyze each scene to determine whether to add or subtract filters or to increase or decrease the intensity of the lamp in the printer. This can be time-consuming and can require more than one attempt or trial print. Additional corrections usually follow the first trial print. Color values may be changed either for internal consistencies within the film or to change an audience's perception of the film. This may be done by "warming up" or "cooling off" certain scenes in the picture. Once the correct balances have been achieved, the answer print of the movie can be made.

From this point, the only thing left in postproduction is release printing. With as many as 1,500 prints now called for in initial print orders, there is no way that the original negative will be risked in running off prints. Instead, duplicate negatives are made and release prints are struck from them. The original negative may then be stored both for posterity and for making future printings.

THE ROLE OF THE PRODUCER

Throughout the course of postproduction the producer should play two very important roles. He must keep a sharp eye on the budget and not allow postproduction expenses to go unchecked. There may be good and valid reasons for the budget to increase but they should be carefully monitored.

In addition, the producer should continue to offer the director and editor an overview on the film itself. The producer will be able to view the film with the unique detachment and objectivity that comes from not working on every scene in the cutting room. He will thus be able to identify those scenes that play too slowly or too quickly or simply do not work. These comments, when offered at this stage of a film's evolution, are as important as any contribution that a producer makes.

In sum, postproduction emerges as an important facet of the creative evolution of a motion picture. While overbudget situations are commonplace in postproduction, the impact on a $10 million budget is generally not great. Moreover, any such budget increase usually occurs with the consent and even the support of the studio or other financing group, as opposed to production where overages are typically viewed with great dismay.

As with so many other parts of filmmaking, there are high-quality editors plying their trade as well as editors better described as mechanics. When practiced at its best, the process of postproduction is an art form. Film editor, sound effects editor, composer, mixer, and others combine to put the finishing touches on a picture, and in the process indelibly stamp the film with their skilled craftsmanship. It is through the combination of their efforts that the old saw lives on: "We'll fix it in postproduction."

III

MARKETING

10

Marketing

Once a picture has been produced, the task of selling remains. The marketing of a film is typically divided into two areas: sales and advertising/publicity. The studios have, in recent years, put both functions under the responsibilities of a single executive, the head of marketing. It is his job to put the often disparate thinking into a single corporate policy and work to maximize the potential return for each of the studio's pictures. This entails positioning the picture in the marketplace with the right campaign, at the right time of year, in the right number of theatres. A tough job in any circumstance, it is one made even more trying by the difficulty of not knowing how rigorous the competition will be at any particular moment. This is the challenge of film distribution and this is the process that the producer must be familiar with if he is to make his presence felt.

THE WORLD OF DISTRIBUTION

Historically, the world of distribution has been a very tough area for the producer to participate in effectively. His views are usually not well received and his efforts to help are seen as little more than interference. In far too many cases, a producer's meeting with the head of distribution will close with the executive rising from his desk, his pinky ring capturing the glint of the afternoon sun, saying, "Trust me, kid. I'll take care of it."

The distribution executive would have you believe that subjectivity is not part of his analysis in the marketing plan for your film and that he is governed only by the business need to maximize film revenues. Generally, he is correct. The theory begins to break down, however, when it is noted that there are so many films released each year that not every one *can* get equal treatment. Since the studio does not have enough money to give each of its films an expensive marketing campaign with all the trimmings, it is necessary to observe carefully the process to ensure that your film is being handled correctly. How well the producer navigates these waters can be a major determining factor in how well a picture ultimately does at the box office.

The situation is not greatly changed if your film is distributed by a smaller company working outside of the aegis of the majors. The same considerations for the campaign, release time, and number of theatres must be faced. Without the benefit of a major studio release, however, one new large problem must be dealt with. That is, the major studios have most of the best theatres in the country tied up under "exclusive" working arrangements, especially during the peak playing times of Christmas and summer. Thus, when a producer works with an independent distributor, he may have the advantage of being able to make his feelings known with some degree of ease, but he will have to suffer with the independent in trying to secure the best theatres at the time of year most beneficial to his picture.

The motion picture industry today is looking with new regard at its marketing leaders. It is curious that the marketing function in motion pictures has never been accorded the respect and status that the creative side of picture-making has received. Typically, the marketer was called in well after the fact and given the assignment of selling an already finished product. More and more, however, marketing men and women are ascending to the highest echelons of corporate life and increasingly their expertise is brought to bear at a much earlier point in a picture's life. Men such as Frank Yablans at MGM-UA, Frank Mancuso at Paramount Pictures, Bob Rehme at New World Pictures, and Terry Semel at Warner Bros. all trace their roots to the marketing area and their influence is a major force in Hollywood today.

Perhaps this is simply a late adjustment to sophisticated marketing techniques imported from other businesses. Perhaps it is because films today are costing unprecedented sums to produce and to market. Whatever the reason, the day of the motion picture marketer is at hand and it behooves the producer to know how to speak his language and to influence his thinking.

MARKETING STRATEGIES—THE PRODUCER

Honesty is the key to a producer's devising a successful marketing strategy for his film. He will have a more intimate knowledge of his picture than any marketing executive, and it is up to him to convert that awareness into a successful sales approach. It is no good to consider your finely crafted art film as having the potential of the next *Star Wars*. Similarly, it is equally fruitless to base a marketing strategy on getting glowing critical acclaim when your film is a rollicking action-adventure movie appealing to a broad international audience. Realism is the order of the day. You should never find yourself so close to the film that you are unable to evaluate objectively its best chance commercially.

THE PRODUCER'S REP

While you may know the makeup of your film better than anyone, you may still need the benefit of expert guidance in formulating a marketing strategy. Producer's representatives provide this assistance.

Individuals who function as producer's reps traditionally come from a background in distribution. They are aware of the major theatres in all parts of the country as well as what distribution terms should be set for any given picture. A rep can be relied on for help in evolving a basic marketing plan, including the media buy and the number of prints in the opening release of the picture. There is so much variation in the method of launching a film that an expert point of view may prove a necessity to the inexperienced producer.

Yet there are drawbacks to hiring a producer's rep. First, it is the producer who must compensate the rep for his services. Studios are unwilling to pick up the cost of a rep since his major occupation will be second-guessing or fighting with it. Rarely will a studio be able to fully satisfy the creators of each of its films. Demands will be made for better theatres, more advertising dollars, a better release date, or any number of other supports for the marketing of their films. Studios try to avoid confrontations in this area and handle all aspects of film marketing on their own. The producer's rep, therefore, is usually perceived as a gadfly whose questions or advice are not wanted.

A good producer's rep must be willing to take chances and put his credibility on the line at all times. When he does function correctly, he is able to furnish the specifics that can rebut arguments advanced by the distribution executives of the studio.

THE BLOCKBUSTER FILM

A handful of films each year will be perceived from their inception as blockbusters and will have the full weight of the studio thrown behind them. They are generally films with superstar actors such as Robert Redford or Clint Eastwood, or films crafted by superstar filmmakers such as Steven Spielberg or George Lucas. If you are fortunate enough to be the producer of such a film, your efforts will be directed to channeling the studio's enthusiasm into constructive directions. More typically, producers are faced with the more difficult task of trying to galvanize a cautious and frequently reluctant studio just to spend the money to give their film a chance in the marketplace.

Long-time distribution man Leo Greenfield believes this is a sound business practice. Speaking from the vantage point of twenty-five years of top sales and distribution jobs in the picture business, Greenfield defends the practice of identifying potential blockbusters: "The big dollars are made on those films that hit the jackpot. Movies like *Jaws, Star Wars, Raiders of the Lost Ark,* and *The Godfather* generate such enormous returns that they justify all the marketing attention. Struggling with less important films can often be very wasteful of both time and money."

THE UNDERDOG FILM

Success may still come to those films that are not the beneficiaries of strong studio support. Movies like *Rocky* or *The Four Seasons* illustrate how the public can make a film a hit without the benefit of studio enthusiasm. In both cases, the producer fought hard for his film and in the end overcame the lack of strong studio support. It should be noted that even pictures as successful as these lost millions of dollars in potential revenue by the studio's placing them in other than the best theatres at terms less favorable than those demanded for their blockbuster pictures.

THE "MIDDLE GROUND" PICTURE

Most pictures can be located near the middle of the studio enthusiasm continuum. They are neither slated to get the blue chip treatment, nor are they scheduled to be unceremoniously dumped on the public without the benefit of advertising and promotion. Within that middle range, there is much that can be done as far as unleashing studio resources and rearranging release patterns. This is where the producer must bear down and put as much pressure on the system as he is able to do. At times, this may be nothing more than yelling louder than anyone else at meetings. At other times, more elaborate strategies may be employed.

CAPRICORN ONE

An example of the dynamic of this process occurred in 1978 when Warner Bros. picked up *Capricorn One* for distribution. As the picture was financed outside the studio, Warners had no production money of their own to recoup and were acting solely as distributors. They acquired the picture to fill a hole in their release schedule during the slack time of February. Their intention was to spend roughly $1 million in launching the film and then sit back and hope for the best. Both the writer-director, Peter Hyams, and I put enormous pressure on the executives of Warners trying to convince them that the company would be better served by releasing it in the summer when film attendance was much greater. By finding allies within the company and by utilizing a growing amount of test data, Warners' thinking began to slowly change. After three successful screenings, the release time was shifted to June and the money allocated to launch the film was upped to $6 million.

None of these battles was won easily since the policy of a February release had already been set. Concerted efforts and unflagging enthusiasm were able to turn the company around. Clearly this was not done to please us. Rather, it was done because the company came to believe in the film itself. Persistence and constant pressure were very much the secrets to effecting the result sought.

CHARIOTS OF FIRE

An even greater success was brought about by producer David Puttnam with his film *Chariots of Fire*. As an arty English film, there were few precedents for successful distribution in America, especially outside the big cities. Warners accepted Puttnam's contention that the film would not be an immediate smash hit with a large audience. They determined that it was a picture that the audience had to find in its own time. Thus, they initially released the picture in only two or three cities. As the film began to garner good critical reviews and good word-of-mouth, they added new theatres. This pattern of adding theatres continued until the Academy Awards when the film was awarded Best Picture and parlayed that triumph into very significant box-office returns.

As a producer, it is important to anticipate whether your film will be perceived as mainstream or as special. In the latter circumstance, you must be prepared to fight as hard as you can to make the studio give the picture a chance. If it doesn't perform, given a fair shot, there is little else that can be done. Ultimately, movies are a business. The studios must endeavor to show a profit with their filmmaking activities. If they have supported your film and the audience has finally rejected it, there is seldom any recourse. Campaigns can be changed, the target audience can be revised, and more money can be pumped into television and other forms of advertising. These steps should be taken. Many a film has turned around after the infusion of new advertising dollars. The role of the producer is to ensure that everything possible to market the film has been done.

MARKETING STRATEGIES—THE EXECUTIVE

Marketing executives are required to form their opinions of a film and their strategies for selling it well before a film is released. Whether or not they are exposed to scripts, casting, stills, or assembled versions of the film, they still must fashion a plan for the marketing of the film. This will include what time of year the picture will open, how many theatres will be in the opening release, and how importantly (i.e., how expensively) the studio will treat this particular film. While it is possible to change policies once they have been formulated, it is unquestionably easier to influence them while they are still taking shape. Preliminary meetings of an exploratory nature are a helpful tool in beginning a dialogue with the marketing people. It is never too early for these conversations. Of course, your film will not be a high priority to the marketing people months before its release. Nonetheless, release schedules are drawn on a yearly basis and it is important to have a say in them.

The business of a studio's determining which of its pictures will be most likely to succeed before audience viewings is very tricky indeed. Naturally, research test results are introduced into the equation as well as reactions from audiences seeing the picture at special screenings. Still, marketing samples are small and statistics show that the guessing game is at best an imperfect science. While it is clear and even understandable that a studio cannot afford to spend $6 to $10 million marketing each of its films, it is not a comforting prospect to learn that your film is not one selected for a big sales push. By withholding advertising dollars, the studio's decision may become a self-fulfilling prophecy. That is, by denying strong advertising and marketing support to a film, a studio may be consigning it to the scrap pile of commercially unsuccessful films without giving it a fair chance. This is not done out of malice, but rather because the studio feels the film has no commercial chance. Often, the producer's voice is the only one raised to protest such actions on the studio's part.

Keep in mind that marketing people, with few exceptions, tend to look to successful precedents. Thus, a James Bond film will have already identified its audience and its selling offers no profound challenge. Far more difficult is the off-center film that has no clear precedent in the marketplace. Positioning *Superman* II or III or *Jaws* II or III presents far different challenges than attempting to sell *Barbarosa*, or *Tender Mercies*, or *The King of Comedy*. Sometimes, with the latter kind of film, the studio will take a deep breath and support the film with advertising and promotion dollars. All too often, however, it will give up at the slightest provocation and inform the producer that the public simply doesn't care for his film.

IMPLEMENTING STRATEGIES: THE PRODUCER AND
THE MARKETING EXECUTIVE

In some respects it is easier for the producer to influence the distribution policy for his film today than in previous times. In an earlier era, responsibility was spread between sales and advertising departments. The new position of head of marketing concentrates responsibility for these two areas into one office. In the past, as Leo Greenfield recalls, there often were jurisdictional disputes: "A distribution man might argue for one theatre in New York City because a picture needed a long run and word-of-mouth. The advertising man would counter: 'For the amount of money I will spend on one theatre, I am better off opening in forty. The advertising cost would be no greater and it is much more cost-effective.' Enter the marketing head. He has to combine a knowledge of advertising with a knowledge of distribution and arbitrate these kinds of disputes."

If the producer's task is to influence the marketing executives toward his thinking about his film, it is important to note that the more clout the producer is able to bring to bear, the greater his chance for success. Sometimes this is measured by the amount of participation the producer has in the film. A producer having 50 percent of the profits of a picture will be perceived as a more important partner of the studio than one having 2½ percent. Likewise, producers with whom the studio has an ongoing relationship will be given more consideration than those who are merely passing through the system. These factors, however, merely define the climate the producer must work in. They do not predetermine the results.

In difficult times, it may be necessary to call in allies to help put pressure on the studio. Actors, directors, agents, lawyers, reps, and even friends can all become advantageously involved in the marketing process. Sometimes studio battles are carried by sheer weight of numbers. Reduced to its simplest terms, the producer should do what he has to do to get his film marketed correctly.

Even when the distribution process is clearly understood by a producer, it remains an onerous task to impose his will upon it. It is far easier to bully or cajole the creative executives at a studio into permitting you to execute a film as you wish than it is to turn a distribution executive in another direction. Instances of out-and-out studio interference in the making of a film are quite rare today. The people putting up the money for a movie have, and probably should continue to have, a bona fide point of view about how that movie should be fashioned. In the vast majority of cases, some semblence of a constructive partnership can be worked out to everyone's relative satisfaction.

In the case of marketing, however, the studio has an over-whelming dominance in the process. Nonetheless, most distribution executives *will* take the time to explain studio policy to you and afford you the opportunity to ask whatever questions you may have. The earlier you begin this discussion, the greater the studio's flexibility will be. If your arguments are cogent and there is time to effect changes in the studio's policy, it is entirely possible that you will be able to effect your desired ends. The most important thing a producer can do is to stay involved in the distribution process. Only then can there be meaningful dialogue between the people who make films and the people who market them.

11

Research

The picture business seems to face more than its share of life-threatening crises. It has successfully withstood the very real economic threats posed by the advent of "talkies," the Great Depression, World War II, the television explosion, the decay of the cities, the gas crunch, and, most recently, cable television and video cassettes. Whether the picture business muddled through these eventful challenges or devised winning strategies is a subject that can generate lively debate. Today, such questions would be resolved by utilizing a tool that has only recently been introduced to motion picture distribution—market research.

Reams of data are now generated by research departments in the major studios. This data purports to give answers and insights on whether films should be made, how they should be sold, and what an audience's awareness of them may be. There is a tendency, at first, to treat this research information as etched in stone. After a closer examination, however, there emerges a tendency to embrace results when they coincide with personal points of view, and reject them when they do not. Since the distribution companies control the market research on films, it is very important to understand the processes involved and where the producer can make himself heard.

THE PURPOSE OF RESEARCH

The goal of research is to bring another voice to the table—the customer who pays his five dollars at the box office. Thus, the point of view of the individual paying for the ticket is added to the perspectives of the sales department, the advertising department, the exhibitor, and the production community.

The researcher strives to be objective in his work. Yet the flaw in this logic is that the researcher is paid by the company distributing the picture and not by an impartial third party. Trained researchers can manipulate results toward any position they wish. In the vast majority of cases, research will thus support the policies of the distribution company. Often it is only the producer who can call a distributor's attention to questionable research and try to redirect the energies of the distributor toward some other goal.

THE HISTORY OF MOVIE RESEARCH

Movie research began by dealing almost exclusively with advertising. Print ads and television ads were tested for their impact on sample audiences. Now, with more sophisticated researchers entering the movie business, more advanced techniques are used. Tracking studies, for example, attempt to measure awareness and attitude penetration for individual films and for competitive product. These studies are part of a new product's introduction to the marketplace similar to studies done by every package goods company in the world. One of the first researchers to use these disciplines in the picture business was Alan Freeman. Originally employed at Bristol Meyers Corporation as a package goods researcher, Freeman became the first professional researcher to make a full-time commitment to the motion picture industry when Bristol Meyers acquired Palomar Pictures, Int'l, a motion picture production company.

MOTION PICTURES AS "PRODUCT"

Freeman embraces the challenge of motion picture research regarding movies as "the ultimate new product." He continues, "We don't have the advantage of an established brand as we would in package goods. We have to conceptualize the product in a number of different ways and present it to the consumer. The consumer has to be motivated to see the films. In that sense, it's all or nothing. You hit a home run or you strike out. You don't see very many singles or doubles today."

CONCEPT TESTING

Although Freeman would like to see his work supported by management and filmmaker alike, he takes exception to the growing tendency to employ research techniques in the production area. In his view, research should not be employed to decide whether to make a film. As Freeman puts it, "I don't think there's any form of concept statement or description that can effectively summarize 120 pages of shooting script."

Concept testing for feature films, on the other hand, can be very effectively employed to isolate the marketing problems that will be encountered down the road. If these problems are large, they may have to be factored into the equation of whether the project as a whole is worth the risks involved. But this is a far different conclusion than deciding on the quality of the script or if the story should be filmed. Some of the industry's most successful films, *Superman,* for example, tested very poorly in advance of the film's being seen. Clearly, hindsight has shown that these results spoke more to the marketing obstacles that had to be overcome rather than to the final decision to make the movie.

There are very good reasons for this. If a film has a terrifically advertisable premise, then it stands to reason that proper advertising can generally cause the film to open successfully, thereby reducing the risk of the investment. Likewise, if a film seems very difficult to advertise, such as Burt Reynolds' film *The End,* a movie about someone dying of cancer, it is clear that it will face an uphill battle to find its place in the market. The great majority of films, however, will fall between the two extremes. In concept testing them, results will be dependent on the language employed by the researchers. Unfortunately, most of the words and phrases associated with motion picture advertising are now so cliched as to be of little real use. Words like "sinister," "evil," or "lurking," when used with a mystery-suspense film, are no longer of any help in gauging audience reactions. Similarly, unusual exploitation films, westerns, or special effects pictures will encounter great difficulties if tested for anything more than future marketing problems. Today's audience is drawn to the theatre not by old cliches but by being convinced that a given film is provocative and entertaining—a most difficult message to convey before the film has come into being.

SNEAK PREVIEWS AND PREVIEW CARDS

Once the film has been assembled, research is customarily employed for sneak previews. In the old days, movie executives claimed to be able to measure the success or failure of a film being previewed by merely listening to the amount of squirming and coughing the audience was doing. Today, more sophisticated techniques have been introduced. Preview cards are handed out to audiences for completion at the theatre. Telephone follow-ups are often utilized to further gauge the audience's reactions. Alan Freeman raises questions about the efficiency of sneak preview cards. With studio executives and filmmakers hovering about in the lobby, a most artificial environment is created for sampling the public's taste. In addition, the process as a whole is susceptible to definite problems. Those audience members who truly hated the film are most likely to leave in disgust without taking the time to fill out their cards. Those that do take the time to fill out cards may not do so seriously or with the detail that the researchers would like.

To get at useful information, the technique of telephone follow-ups should be employed. Such calls are made to audience members by trained interviewers within 48 hours of the preview. Once away from the theatre, and given the perspective of a little time and distance, preview audience members have tended to be less favorably disposed toward the movie and have tended to get closer to their real evaluation of the film.

RELIABILITY

Motion picture research as a whole has proven to be far more predictive of success or failure than comparable data for package goods. In the vernacular of the researcher, testing in the motion picture industry has proven very stable; that is, testing and retesting tends to produce the same results. There are apparently good reasons for this. Moviegoers, members of the 18- to 49-year-old population, represent about one out of three people, and as a group, tend to be relatively homogeneous. In addition, unlike many other consumer products, there is very little difficulty getting man-on-the-street interviews. While the average citizen may have little to say about a particular brand of coffee or toothpaste, he is generally quite enthusiastic about participating in a research study having to do with motion pictures. These reasons alone contribute to the inherent stability of test results. According to Freeman, advertising campaigns that tested badly in his research were followed by unsuccessful picture openings.

It is worth noting that unlike elections that may be decided by fractions of percentages, test results for films look to measure comparatively huge differences. No one is particularly concerned whether a film is going to gross $1.2 million or $1.5 million. Rather, the swing of $1 million versus $10 million or even $50 million is what research hopes to ascertain. At times, as with *Star Wars,* the early testing may be singularly inconclusive. Testing on that film revealed that there would be major problems convincing people that the film could appeal to a broad audience. Eight pages in *Time* magazine heralding the film as the year's best movie went a long way toward overcoming that particular marketing problem. Such identification of marketing problems is what motion picture research should be all about.

WORD-OF-MOUTH

Of course, above all else, you hope audiences will love your movie and will tell their friends to see it. If they do, then you will have achieved the much sought-after commodity—word-of-mouth. Few have taken the time to quantify precisely what this term really means. As Freeman points out, an enormously successful and popular film like *Star Wars* will inspire 50 to 60 percent of its audience to come away saying, "This is one of the best films I've ever seen." If each of those individuals convinces one person to see the film, then the best result achievable will be to halve the audience. If each person were able to convince two people to see the picture, you would repeat the original audience size. But, if you look three or four weeks down the road, and multiply the original 50 percent by four, a geometric progression is seen to develop. This is what makes word-of-mouth work. It takes time, especially when you scale down from a film like *Star Wars* to a less successful picture.

By understanding the dynamic of word-of-mouth, advertising strategies can be developed to meet the particular problems of the picture at hand. An understanding of this process, for example, may prompt you to urge that the distribution company hold back advertising dollars until the second or third weeks of the campaign in order to allow word-of-mouth to begin to be effectively felt.

THE COMPETITION

Just as with a poker hand, it is not sufficient to pay attention only to your own situation. It is at least as important to try to get a fix on the competition. In the movie industry, such information is very hard to come by. It is very difficult to objectively assess the quality of your competitor's product. Generally, the best you are able to do is to identify the big spenders, or those films that seem destined to spend major sums of money in advertising and publicity to gain some foothold in the market. Although this information will not tell you which films will finally appeal to the largest segments of the audience, it will tell you which competitive films are likely to be in the market for the long haul, well-supported by advertising dollars.

THE ROLE OF THE PRODUCER

As a producer, it is most unlikely that you will be able to finance your own research. You will, therefore, have to come to grips with the research data developed by the distribution company— whether or not it is supportive of your film. You may be able to get the distribution company to do additional research if you believe the first results are either in error or are misleading because of some factor. Usually if you work with the research department of a distributor, courtesies of this kind will be extended to you. It requires persistence and an open mind. The latter quality is necessary because there are times when research will produce critical information that can shape both the campaign and the commercial results of the picture.

OH GOD!

A good example of what research can do is found in a film that Alan Freeman worked on, *Oh God!*. Warner Bros. studio management had very little confidence in the film. Their estimates of film rentals ranged from $3 million to $7 million. Research showed the following: When you told the story from the perspective of God, rather than the assistant supermarket manager, you had a far stronger movie. From that perspective, people identified with the situation. "Maybe it'll be me He'll contact," they reasoned. Telling the story from the perspective of the supermarket manager, on the other hand, made it sound like low comedy, or a picture that had no substance to it.

The campaign was adjusted to take into account the research.

The perspective of God became the dominant motif in print, television, and trailers. When the picture previewed well, the research data was presented to the Warner Bros. management, who supported the marketing people. "Go spend the money you need to get this picture open," was the new management mandate. In so doing, they provided the marketers with an advertising budget that exceeded what their original expectation of film rentals had been. Their confidence was ultimately borne out by the box-office result. This also points out the crucial role of a supportive management if research is to be effective.

In many cases, research is not considered a marketing tool as it was with *Oh God!*. According to Freeman, "In most situations, research is a tool, off to the side, to be used when it is convenient. It is too often there to buttress someone's point of view rather than to challenge someone's assumptions."

CAPRICORN ONE

Research also played a dramatic role in convincing the distribution company to reverse its original thinking regarding the release of *Capricorn One*. Working with the studio's research department, I encouraged them to do more and more testing to bolster my point of view that the picture should be released with far greater support than the studio contemplated. Gradually enough data was accumulated to convince the studio to change its release date and the kinds of theatres it would book the picture into.

In that case, the head of research for the studio developed an affinity for the film. Although he owed his primary allegiance to the studio which paid his salary, he nonetheless was able to enthusiastically support *Capricorn One*'s chances at the box office. Finding an ally anywhere in the distribution machinery of a studio is always a boon to the producer. This case was no exception. His convictions, supported by the data he developed, were an invaluable asset in assisting the filmmakers in their efforts to get the studio to see the film as they saw it.

MPAA RESEARCH

The Motion Picture Association of America (MPAA) pays for many research studies which are often treated as unassailable by the distribution companies. Alan Freeman, however, raises some interesting questions about the validity of their findings.

The MPAA has reported at length, for example, the average age of the most frequent moviegoers. Their data shows this group to be between 15 and 25 years old. This statistic has, in turn, shaped the kinds of films that are made.

But are the MPAA's statistics accurate? Freeman thinks not. Every tracking study that he has undertaken has had to factor in young peoples' overreporting of movie-going. Five percent of the under 17's, for example, generally report they have seen movies that haven't yet been released or previewed. In many cases, they may not even have started production. Perhaps they were confused about the title. But why would it always be the under 17's who were confused? In addition, research has shown that it is very difficult to establish a normative data base or produce meaningful comparisons when testing this age level because they want to see everything. Finally, if you remove from the MPAA statistics independently made films and test only product from the major studios, you will find that the influence of young people diminishes. Movie attendance, without allowing for independently made films, will be much more evenly spread.

Freeman tends to look at the data a little differently. Age, by itself, is a false statistic to focus upon, because lifestyle, not age, is the most important determinant, according to his analysis. A person 21, married, with two young children, is going to have very little disposable income and very little free time to go to the movies. But someone 28, single, and employed in a good job has no domestic responsibility and has ample time to see a lot of movies. In his mind, it is the stage of the life cycle that is critical, not age per se.

THE CONSUMER TODAY: A SELECTIVE MOVIEGOER

What else does research tell us in an overall sense about today's consumer? With every passing year, he is becoming increasingly price-conscious. As movie admission prices climb, he wants more and more reassurance before he parts with his five dollars. Since he has come to feel that the price is somewhat exorbitant, he looks for assurances that he will have a satisfying experience for his money. Whether that experience is fundamentally escapist or emotional is not the most important issue. It must be satisfying.

As a consumer, he looks for these assurances from three sources: word-of-mouth, advertising, or critics. Movies that were unheralded at their opening, like *Arthur* or *Airplane*, demonstrate the profound impact of word-of-mouth and good notices. Thousands of people were persuaded to see those movies based on what they had heard about them. This phenomenon produced greater business in the second and third weeks of their runs than in the first week. Both films got better notices from the critics than their distributors anticipated. Particularly in the case of television critics, this has become a vital link to the consuming public. Such reviewers offer their comments in the intimacy of the audience's own residence. While no one presumes omniscience on the part of the television critic, the public is only too happy to say, "If I agree with the critic 90 percent of the time, at least I can avoid wasting my five dollars so often."

This trend toward more selective movie-going has been emerging for some time. With the consumer's need for reassurance, an advertising man would tell you that this is the time to be very aggressive. If the public is becoming more selective, spend more money, not less. In motion picture terms, this translates into spending $5 or $6 million on advertising, and not $2 or $3 million. But the major studios seem to have great difficulty adapting to the new reality. If anything, their actions have been characterized by a cautionary attitude not at all in keeping with the seeming need for aggressive spending.

THE STUDIO AND MARKETING RESEARCH

With audiences demanding reassurances before they venture out to the theatre, and with studios reluctant to spend freely on the release of every film, the producer is in something of a bind. Market research may not always provide the answer. It is a sad but realistic comment on the motion picture business that unless the studio is already enthusiastic about a film, it will probably not do exhaustive market research to assist it in the film's marketing. Thus, the research for a film like *Superman* wound up doing in excess of 10,000 interviews, while movies that carried less studio hope tended to do less than 1,000. With a small sample to work from, the results can prove too unstable to have much meaning. Yet you will be hard-pressed to try to get more market research from a company that is lukewarm about the commercial prospects of your picture. The final choices still belong to the studio.

In the final analysis, given the introduction of cable television, and ever-higher prices at the box office, it is increasingly incumbent on the marketers to be able to position a picture in a way that is distinctive from what can be seen for free on television. The film must be perceived as unique relative to other competitive motion pictures, and compelling in and of itself. Marketing should make you want to see the picture, and, in the words of Alan Freeman, it's "going to require a lot more imagination, and a lot better advertising and research than we're getting now."

Both Freeman's remarks and common sense indicate that research can offer a great deal to the business of marketing motion pictures. What is trickier to get at is the ultimate objectivity and validity of the results finally obtained. It is perhaps to be expected that something less than total objectivity will be forthcoming, given the circumstances of motion picture distribution. Yet if the ultimate consumer, the film audience, is heard, only good can result. Research constitutes a tool of growing importance in the picture business and one that should be understood by both the producer and the studio. At a minimum, it demands an awareness and an instinct for how to use research to your advantage. With these assets in your arsenal, research can be a most valuable tool.

12

Motion Picture Advertising

The area of motion picture advertising is one of surprising uncertainty and confusion. It is clear that advertising is designed to attract patrons to the box office. But which patrons? And how do the patrons make up their minds what they want to see?

There is remarkably little agreement among the professionals on the answers to these questions. With rare exceptions it is very difficult for distribution executives to guide advertising people into the identification of a specific market segment for a specific film. It is equally difficult to find agreement on the type of advertising that is thought to be the appropriate selling tool on any given film. The usual rule is that there will be as many disparate views as there are people in the room. Market research has been introduced to the process, ostensibly to clarify and objectify the problem. Whether the research does that or simply adds another dimension of confusion is disputable.

Advertising has at least four clear purposes. First, it should create an awareness of the picture in the minds of the audience. Second, it should provide the audience with information about the film. Increasingly important to today's audience, it should also point out the qualities that make the film unique. Finally, advertising must function as a persuader—a means to induce the audience to make up its mind to see a particular film. A great deal of money is spent in the achieving of these four aims.

Distributors customarily allocate anywhere from $1 million to $5 million to advertise a film. Some of this money goes for the creation of radio, television, print, and trailer advertising. The bulk of the spending, however, is earmarked for the purchase of commercial time on radio and television or space in the print medium. These vast sums required to advertise a film today put a high premium on the advertising materials and the role that the producer should play in helping create them.

THREE INTERESTED PARTIES

The three principal groups involved in the creation of advertising materials are the studio (or other financing entity), the filmmakers (usually the producer and director), and the service organization selected to do the actual work. It is very hard to keep these three factions thinking in like terms because within each faction there may be internecine disagreements. Were this not enough, the needs of foreign markets may place a further constraint on the process of coming up with the best advertising for the picture. The beautiful, tasteful ad that is much to your liking may have to be sacrificed in favor of an action-oriented ad suitable for foreign territories.

With all these forces impacting on the process of motion picture advertising, it is doubly disturbing that there is so little agreement about the very philosophy of motion picture advertising. Many will argue that print ads merely provide the time and place of the showing of a film. Others contend that television carries the real persuaders that induce people to make up their minds which movies they will go to see. A more logical position might be that each aspect of a campaign—print, television, radio, or trailers—should reinforce every other aspect so that the public is swept along into the movie theatre. Even on this point there is no real unanimity within the industry. Many pictures are marketed with splinter campaigns seemingly appealing with equal degrees of enthusiasm and concentration to different segments of the market.

STUDIO ADVERTISING

In an earlier era of the motion picture business, advertising campaigns were created within each studio by the advertising/publicity department. The chief executive of that department, working with the head of the studio, fashioned a campaign that he thought did justice to the film and stood the best chance of attracting a wide audience. He had copywriters to assist in finding the right copy to support the ad concept as well as artists to execute the graphic designs. The overall approach was originated within his department, under his control.

Nowadays, the advertising/publicity head is more like a corporate manager who picks and chooses outside service organizations or vendors to come up with the campaigns that will be ultimately employed. In-house capability is a thing of the past. The producer seeking to help exploit his film must come to terms with this new corporate structure. He must be mindful of the high degree of anxiety that surrounds the advertising/publicity executives today and must work within that system. Within the studio framework, if a picture is a hit in today's market, the head of production of the studio generally rushes to take full credit. If the picture is a failure, it is instantly blamed on the campaign emanating from the advertising department. This kind of no-win situation is not conducive to the creation of a healthy climate where the exchange of ideas and concepts is free flowing and mutually beneficial.

EARLY ADVERTISING AND PUBLICITY

At the outset, during the production of the film, the producer must ride herd on the unit photographer and the unit publicist. In the case of the former, the producer's help is often required to intercede with the stars of the film to pose for stills. Many stars have the right to approve stills in which they appear as a matter of contract. The checking of the unit publicist's copy can also be a very important task. He will be finding phrases to describe the action and theme of the film which all too often find their way into publicity releases and finally into reviews and feature stories turned out by journalists here and abroad. If the publicist misperceives or misdescribes the picture, it may prove most difficult to eliminate the offending copy unless it is checked at the source before it leaves location.

The production period of a film is not too early to choose a logo which can accompany all publicity and other releases pertaining to the film. There have been very few instances of memorable logos in recent years. Motion pictures like *Jaws, Close Encounters of the Third Kind,* and *Heaven Can Wait* do come to mind as examples of successful choices in this regard. Often the studio resists locking in a single logo at this early stage for fear that its appeal will be to a too-narrow audience segment. Studios prefer to roll this problem forward until a date closer to the film's release. This fear or insecurity from the studio should be counteracted wherever possible by the producer.

Another area of concern during photography is the choice of whether to hire a special still photographer. Often the name of a celebrated photographer will be instrumental in getting a picture published in *People, Time,* or *Newsweek* magazines. Yet the best unit photographers can certainly match the special photographers in skill and results. The one advantage to a special photographer is that he will not be at the mercy of the budget and the film's director. He will not be limited in time and lighting by the movements of the director. His angles will not be controlled by where the director chooses to set his cameras. Instead, the special photographer will be treated to a preplanned session in which his material will be lit and shot for advertising purposes alone. This allows for a vastly different degree of creative results and works in favor of paying the extra money to retain the services of a first-rate special photographer for a limited time on all pictures.

SELECTING A SERVICE ORGANIZATION

Most helpful to the producer and the studio in working with the special photographer and in all facets of the preparation of advertising materials is the early selection of a service organization or vendor to physically prepare the materials and supervise the campaign from the earliest stages onward. Studios tend to resist putting such organizations on a picture as early as production because they are not sure, in most cases, how enthusiastic they will be about the finished film. In addition, they are faced with the very real problem of marketing a year's worth of product before the picture in production will be released. Here again it is the producer who must wave the banner for his picture, and must drum up the necessary support to implement these early marketing strategies. One useful direction to proceed in is to guide the studio toward the selection of an organization capable of developing and coordinating all of the pieces of a campaign, from logo, to copy, full color master print, black and white master print, teaser trailer, trailer, and radio and television spots. One such company is Intralink Film Graphic Design of Los Angeles whose president, Anthony Goldschmidt, is one of the foremost creative forces in today's world of motion picture advertising. His company, Intralink, offers an integrated and unified approach to all the pieces of an advertising campaign for a film.

THE PRODUCER'S INPUT

A producer has to determine whether he should tell an organization like Intralink the direction he has in his mind, or send them out to come back with whatever concepts seem appropriate to them. On the one hand, as a producer, you don't want them to spin their wheels in pursuit of a theme that is too far off the mark to be usable. On the other hand, you don't want to impose constraints that might tend to inhibit creative thinking. Goldschmidt, very clear on his preference, says, "It is always more helpful when people put their cards on the table. We strive to have a meaningful dialogue with the producer during which each of our concepts can be discussed." Goldschmidt doesn't look to the producer to do his design work for him. Rather, he wants to hear what elements the producer feels should be captured in the advertising. "At that point," continues Goldschmidt, "we have a pretty good sense of, not an ad, but his feelings about what he thinks he has to sell. We feel that that kind of dialogue is very meaningful before we start work."

The work process may mean very different things to the studio, the filmmakers, and the service organization. Many filmmakers have a contractual right to "advertising consultation." This vague term is generally defined by the muscle or clout of the filmmaker involved. For the neophyte producer, advertising consultation may mean being shown a piece of art work by the studio. If the filmmaker says, "I don't like it," the studio may say, "You've just been consulted." The same technique is not about to be employed with a Blake Edwards, a Mel Brooks, a Steven Spielberg, or any other established filmmaker. With them, the studio is forced to deal with the very active hand they take in the marketing of the picture.

The more experienced the filmmaker, the more realistic he tends to be about the movie he has made. No one starts out to make a bad film. Some end up less successful than others. The experienced producer generally tries to maximize the return on what he has and in furtherance of that goal tends to be objective and realistic in the selling of the picture.

Within these parameters, the service organization often has to walk a very fine line. The studio is paying their bill on that film as well as other films in the future. Nonetheless, strong filmmakers have a large voice in who is hired to work on their pictures. The service organization rarely takes sides between the filmmaker and the studio. Recognizing that both parties have strong vested interests in seeing the film succeed, the service organization often seeks a compatible middle ground. At times, this can impose an onerous political burden upon the service organization. Most vendors accept this as part of the job, hoping only that the situation does not become so exacerbated that good creative work won't be able to be accomplished.

THE ADVERTISING CAMPAIGN

THE TARGET AUDIENCE

The threshold question that anyone fashioning a campaign must come to grips with is a definition of the audience that the campaign is trying to reach. Goldschmidt, who feels very strongly that the process of targeting a film's audience is essential to all that follows in a campaign, says, "You open your film to your target audience and then hang in there with it and hope that the target audience you've found feels that they've gotten their money's worth." This theory pertains no matter whether the film is *Texas Chainsaw Massacre, Chariots of Fire,* or *Gandhi.* In each case, the advertising should not be compromised. Once the target audience has been identified, the campaign should be directed at it with resolve and dedication. The resistance that may have to be overcome will be the studio's nervousness about narrowing the appeal for the film. The producer can be very helpful in leading the studio to identify the target audience and to direct the primary advertising approach to reach this market segment.

As Goldschmidt so aptly puts it, "The first rule of thumb on motion picture advertising is that you can't buy word-of-mouth." You must attract those paying customers who will enjoy the product you have put together for them, and who will then go out and tell other like-minded people that this film is solid entertainment for them. In that regard, it matters not whether they are attracted to a film on cannibalism or a film extolling the virtues of human nature. Accurately depict what the film is about in your advertising and you can never go too far wrong. Try to describe it as something-for-everyone, on the other hand, and you can often find your film slipping between the cracks and disappearing from public sight forever.

THE ADVERTISING MATERIAL

Once the target audience has been identified, the preparation of the advertising material can begin. There is no right and wrong to what constitutes a good advertisement. Certain product seems to require one approach while other films dictate something altogether different. Perhaps consistent with his target audience thinking, Goldschmidt adopts a simple tenet for his advertising efforts. As he puts it, "Less is more. I believe that the least memorable campaigns are those that promise something for everyone." This need not always mean a minimalist art and copy concept. By way of illustration, Goldschmidt refers to the campaign for the Mel Brooks film *Blazing Saddles*. The art work in that campaign was extremely "busy," like the picture itself. Goldschmidt analogized *Blazing Saddles* to a banana split. It had three scoops of ice-cream, chocolate sauce, strawberries, cherries, nuts, whipped cream, and bananas. The campaign, in turn, was representative of the film.

THE COPYLINE

In principle, the copyline that is evolved for the campaign should work as a cohesive unit with the art. If this interaction is successful, then the result is that the whole is greater than the sum of the parts in the ad. Less successful ads demonstrate the problems of the art and the copy pulling in separate directions. When a good ad works, the marriage between art and copy will not seem to be a redundancy, but rather a close and effective interaction.

TELEVISION SPOTS

It should be noted that although most studios tend to place considerable emphasis on the value of television advertising today and tend to downgrade the importance of print, there is another side to this discussion because of the enormous competition in television today. Generally speaking, a television spot for a film is little more than an assemblage of scenes from the picture with some narration. These spots must compete against corporations that spend hundreds of thousands of dollars to produce one 30-second production number that the audience will remember for days to come. Not only that, these same corporations will put up millions of dollars to assure that the television audience will see these commercials many, many times in the expectation that repetitive viewings will firmly implant the message and the imagery in the audiences' minds. It is not an easy task to compete effectively in this marketplace.

One thing is clear. The demographics of television are so detailed that it is possible to spend advertising dollars in a reasonably effective manner. Once the target audience has been identified, it is certainly possible to buy advertising time on those shows that the target audience is watching. The choice of which shows to advertise on has become almost a science, albeit one greatly limited by the funds available to implement the plan.

"FREE INK": PUBLICITY/PROMOTION

One area that is much neglected in today's market is old-fashioned promotion. Free ink, as it used to be called, is derived from promotional acts designed to capture the public's attention by making inroads on the news media. Certain producers such as Allan Carr, Robert Evans, and Peter Guber have kept this art alive. By and large, however, producers of today and the advertising-publicity departments seem less than disposed to concentrate on this form of marketing. With the cost of television time today, it is surprising that more producers haven't seen fit to reacquaint themselves with the traditional devices of the promotional-minded salesman.

As with all other facets of motion pictures, the costs of film advertising continue to mount. Numerous suppliers on both coasts hold themselves out as being able to solve all the puzzles of motion picture advertising. But like so many things in life, there has to be some agreement on the questions before there can be any unanimity on the answers. There remains an uneasy truce between the market-research-oriented executives and the old seat-of-the-pants executives who believe they'll know what is right as soon as they see it.

THE ROLE OF THE PRODUCER

For the producer seeking to assist in the marketing of his film, advertising is a critical component in the mix. The more knowledgable the producer is and the more aggressive and active a role he plays in the process, the more his cause will be served. At a minimum, the producer should be able to bring to the table a sure knowledge of what his film is about and who will be most likely to respond to it. If those concepts can be kept clearly in mind throughout the wrangling that normally accompanies the selection of an advertising campaign, the producer will have taken a giant step toward arriving at the best selling approach for his film.

13

Foreign Distribution

A producer should be well acquainted with the foreign distribution of motion pictures. Not only do revenues from areas outside the United States and Canada constitute approximately 50 percent of the world's theatrical gross revenues, but the distributors in these foreign territories will, under the right circumstances, put up cash guarantees for distribution rights which can be used to finance the movie that is being licensed. This boot-strap method of raising production funds is often employed by the producer operating outside the aegis of the major studios. Either he or a qualified sales representative will assemble a package with the elements necessary to make the foreign distributor agreeable to funding a film he has not seen. This market is very sophisticated and considerable expertise is necessary to successfully satisfy the needs of the many different active buyers.

GUARANTEES

There are two kinds of guarantees that foreign distributors will advance. One is the aforementioned advance made on the basis of the assembled package, before the film is produced. The other is an advance after the film has been produced and is ready for exploitation. In both cases, the distributor is advancing a sum of money against the producer's share of the proceeds from the film's distribution in his territory.

Typically, if a producer were to receive an advance of $250,000, the distributor would be entitled to the first $500,000 in rentals (to recoup his advance and pay his distribution expenses), and

177

then additional monies would be split on a negotiated percentage between the distributor and the producer. The additional rentals are termed "overages" and are, of course, of prime importance in the structure of a deal.

CROSS-COLLATERALIZATION VERSUS TERRITORIAL SALES

Once films are produced, there are critical distinctions between how major companies and independents distribute. The major company releases its pictures under its own banner throughout the world, lumping its profits and losses into one statement. Thus, if a film performed very successfully in France, for example, but proved a big disappointment in Germany, the losses in the latter situation might more than offset the profits arising out of France. This method of accounting is known as cross-collateralization, which means offsetting profits against losses and arriving at a net amount. This is far less advantageous to a third-party profit participant such as a producer than if the foreign results were not cross-collateralized but rather left to stand on their own. Thus, as in the previous example, if the picture was a big earner in France, those monies would go directly into the film's gross receipts; whereas, the losses incurred in Germany would stand by themselves and would not be deducted from any other country's receipts. This method is an alternative to cross-collateralization and is known as territorial sales. It has proven to be an enormous boon for producers operating as independents, outside the studio system.

In personal terms, *Capricorn One,* which I produced for Lord Lew Grade's English production company, was presold to territories all over the world. He received some $2.5 million in guarantees plus a formula for overages in the event the film performed well in any territory. In actual fact, the film did exceedingly well in some territories such as Japan, Scandinavia, and several South American countries. Despite a lot of hard work, it proved to be a disappointment in such important areas as Germany, France, Italy, and Great Britain. Had he offset the gains from the countries that did well by the losses from the rest of the world, foreign distribution would have produced a negative overall result. By selling territorially, however, the picture registered a decidedly positive cash result from foreign distribution.

It hasn't taken producers long to understand the value of not cross-collateralizing foreign sales results. To accomplish this end, as a rule, it is necessary to distribute outside the major companies. Previously this was not available as an option to the same extent that it is today. In part this stems from the new financial sources that producers have tapped today, and in part it comes from the new disposition of the major companies to welcome financial partners as a means of sharing the risk. However the opportunity arose, it has afforded producers a tremendously significant avenue to realize monies from distribution that was formerly not open to them.

FOREIGN SALES REPRESENTATIVES

For the producer who has spent a lifetime working in the foreign arena, raising money from foreign distributors holds no mystery. For the rest of us, it can be a bewildering maze of foreign countries and strange names. To bridge this gap, many foreign sales organizations have sprung into being in the past years. Most are qualified sales representatives who are able to make the necessary deals on a producer's behalf. A few seek not only to sell foreign markets but also to supervise the actual distribution process on the behalf of their clients. The Producers Sales Organization, PSO, is such a company.

Under its founder and president, Mark Damon, PSO has grown to a position of strength and importance within the industry. Damon began his career as a promising young actor and ended up in Europe working as a leading man. He branched out into writing, producing, and directing before finally turning to distribution. Operating initially from Italy, Damon came into contact with the other distributors of the world before returning to the

United States. Once back in the States, he identified a need for independent overseas distribution and formed PSO.

Damon is quick to point out the term "foreign sales" is very much a misnomer today. In earlier years in the motion picture industry, the major companies might elect not to try selling certain films abroad, and the producer himself might sell what he could, for whatever he could get. Today, very rarely is a film *sold* to a foreign distributor. Instead, the foreign distributor is granted a license to theatrically exploit the film within his territory. As Damon adds, a producer's responsibility does not stop here. "It's simply not enough to take a picture and give it to a foreign distributor. You have an investment in the picture. You have put time into it and created a project that you hope will be well distributed, not only domestically, but also overseas. It should continue to be marketed, promoted, coordinated and distributed properly by the people who are the foreign licensees."

A company like PSO will furnish the licensee with materials to promote the product, will coordinate the release with them, including the kinds of terms they should get and the pattern of release of the picture, and will provide them with ways to publicize the film. Such a liaison service is intended to extract maximum dollars from the picture's foreign distribution by seeing that the marketing strategies are implemented. On this level, a company like PSO is really more of a distribution company than it is a sales organization. Its principal distinction from a classic distribution company is that it does not in fact release the films and does not have to bear the overhead costs attendant to such a business. It supervises distribution and utilizes the auspices of national distributors on a territorial basis.

Among the advantages to using national distributors instead of the foreign branches of the American major companies is the follow-through within each country. The major companies can do very well in the first-run key cities within a territory. Their offices are there and the wealth of their experience is derived from the key cities. They are not as successful in moving their product into the second, third, and fourth runs in the provinces. Local distributors have proven far more effective at taking in this last third of a film's potential revenue. Further, a national distributor who has had to put up a healthy guarantee to obtain distribution rights tends to be more creative in finding ways to market the film in order to recoup his investment and hopefully turn a profit. He is far more inclined to take chances in distribution, such as changing campaigns to suit local tastes, if he thinks this may produce greater returns. Major studio exchanges, on the other hand, tend to be more cautious about committing additional funds to a foreign campaign unless the film is an instant success.

What a sales representative, PSO or otherwise, promises to deliver are guarantees from the major territories of the world. It would be easy sailing if such guarantees were payable in full when the deals were made. Unfortunately, this is not the case. In the event the rights are negotiated before the film is produced, a down payment will be made together with the distributor's promise to pay the balance when the film is delivered to him. This promise, in the form of a contract signed by the distributor, is typically taken to a bank, which will provide the producer with something less than the face amount of the commitment—a process called discounting. These are the funds the producer uses to physically produce his picture. Either the sales representative or any of a number of attorneys can be very helpful in arranging for the contracts from foreign distributors to be discounted and converted to cash to help finance production.

A company like PSO does approximately 85 percent of its business at the three big film markets each year. These gatherings, at Milan (Mifed), Cannes, and Los Angeles (the American Film Market), bring together film buyers from all over the world. They see finished product and presentations for all kinds of would-be films. In the heat of a competitive atmosphere, there is often frenzied buying by foreign distributors which can mean the difference between getting a picture financed or seeing hopes go down the drain. Much of the excitement generated at these festivals will trickle down to the exhibitors and thereby give the producer a big assist in the ultimate selling of his picture.

DOMESTIC VERSUS FOREIGN SUCCESS

In the early days of PSO, a number of films were handled whose foreign grosses far exceeded their domestic grosses. Such so-so domestic film performers as *The Final Countdown*, *The Wanderers*, and *Phantasm* proved to be large grossers in the overseas market. Moreover, by selling territorially, producers were able to realize additional monies even though the results of their films were spotty to say the least. A film like *Endless Love*, for example, returned far more to its producer than it would have had it been released by a major. In the latter situation, its losses would have erased its gains. Territorial sales, however, allowed it to become a fairly important hit in the overseas marketplace.

THE FOREIGN MARKET

Insofar as gauging the importance of different foreign territories, it should be noted that approximately seven countries comprise nearly 50 percent of the world's gross, outside of the United States and Canada. Although the order of importance is subject to yearly fluctuations, these countries are Germany, France, Japan, United Kingdom, Australia, Italy, and Spain. Tides within each country will account for movement up and down the scale of total film revenues. In France, for example, the Mitterand government cut back on the number of feature films shown on the state-controlled television network. This produced less entertaining television and resulted in an upswing in theatrical film attendance. In Australia, the advent of color television brought about a decided drop in theatrical attendance. As the novelty of color television began to wear off, attendance at the movie theatres took a pronounced upturn.

And today the marketplace is experiencing the impact of home video in a major way. Whether it will develop an altogether different audience, as some believe, or instead erode the theatrical film audience is too early to tell. Indications are that there will be a definite drop in theatrical admissions wherever home video makes inroads into the consumer market.

The producer who has a film in his mind has to be able to assess its comparative value in the foreign marketplace. What kinds of movies does this market prefer? Can all foreign distribution be lumped into a single set of preferences? Are there specific actors or directors who command loyal followings abroad? Are there some kinds of pictures that may do well in America but have proven anathema abroad? These and other like questions should be answered by the producer trying to exploit his film property to the fullest in foreign markets.

FOREIGN AUDIENCES

It is difficult to assess accurately the film tastes of foreign audiences. They tend to change as rapidly and with as little consistency as those of American audiences. In general, audiences in France like political films and police thrillers, whereas audiences in Germany generally do not. Most nonmusical spectacle pictures that do well in the United States tend also to do well abroad. Films like *Raiders of the Lost Ark* and *Superman* fit into this category. Visual comedies such as those made by Mel Brooks tend to do very well abroad whereas sophisticated dialogue comedies tend not to travel well outside the United States. Sentimental films do very well in the Latin countries, Japan, and the United Kingdom. In Germany and Northern Europe, they do very badly. Action-adventure films, once the mainstay of foreign distribution, now have to have some saleable element or hook to do even respectable business. The foreign audiences seem to have had their fill of medium-sized action thrillers and will refuse to support them at the box office unless some other aspect of the film captures their fancy.

Even casting has become a trickier pursuit than it was several years ago. Gone are the days when any recognizable Hollywood name would be enough to sell a film abroad. With more exposure to American product has come a greater degree of sophistication and a greater amount of discrimination. Venerable movie stars are still respected overseas, perhaps more so than in America, but not to the same extent as they were in the comparatively recent past.

There is virtually no female star who commands an important following abroad. Barbra Streisand has little if any of the cachet she brings to movies in this country, stemming from the fact that musical films do not export well. The American-ness of her comedy which has made her a huge star in this country has probably worked against her abroad. Likewise Meryl Streep and Jane Fonda are certainly recognizable to foreign audiences, but they tend not to be large draws overseas. Foreign distributors will pick up their films for distribution because of the importance of their names. But hopes for box-office bonanzas do not run high simply because these names appear in the cast.

Very rarely an American will achieve uncommon prominence within some specific national group. This isolated acclaim has been heaped on Jerry Lewis by the French. His films are treated as historic milestones and the grosses reflect his popularity. Being adopted in this manner by a foreign market is a rare occurrence. Charles Bronson enjoyed this kind of popularity abroad for a time. Others have as well, but not often.

Certain directors also command a large following in the major foreign markets. As with the actor list, these names may not coincide with those on the list of "hot" directors for the companies in this country. Certain directors such as Spielberg, Coppola, or Lucas are now so well established that their names know no boundaries, national or international. Other names are less obvious. Sergio Leone is considered one of the greatest directorial stars of all time by the foreign distributors, and ultimately by the foreign audiences. The late Sam Peckinpah is an example of an American director whose name was extremely meaningful to those in the foreign market. The popularity of directors and actors in this area is a direct result of previous pictures that succeeded in countries outside the United States. Sometimes, as with Sam Peckinpah's *Convoy*, foreign grosses greatly exceeded domestic returns, further adding to the marketability of Peckinpah's name overseas.

Very few producers achieve this kind of star status in the foreign market. Producer-directors George Lucas and Francis Coppola are certainly on the list. Perhaps Richard Zanuck and David Brown, Ray Stark, Dino De Laurentiis, and maybe David Puttnam might be on such a list. Several overseas successes are all that it really takes to become enshrined in this kind of pantheon.

The importance of being part of these lists signifies a good track record for the raising of money from foreign sources. Along with a track record must be added a screenplay with a subject interesting to a foreign market. With these ingredients in place it is possible either to raise money before production or to realize monies during foreign distribution. As the names on these potential lists are in flux at any moment in time, it may serve the new producer well to seek the advice and counsel of a qualified foreign sales representative. He should be able to quickly assess the marketability of the package you have assembled in the markets that he services. Second opinions may prove necessary, but the answers can be obtained with a reasonable degree of accuracy.

SHOWMANSHIP

It is worth noting that even with territorial sales of a motion picture, the producer is well advised to shepherd his film through the opening engagements in the important foreign territories whenever this can be done. Foreign distributors are generally delighted to get all the help they can in opening American pictures. By coordinating a visit to the territory, if possible accompanied by the star and director of the picture, with the local distributor, considerable free ink and media time can be obtained. The more of an event the opening can be turned into, the more chance the picture has to succeed. Showmanship is not a commodity which stops at America's borders. It may require initiative on the producer's part to pull this off, but it should be seen as part of his responsibilities in the marketing of the film. After the ink on the contracts has dried, there is often no one but the producer left to supervise distribution and to promote the film.

Another quirk in efforts to secure prefinancing guarantees from foreign markets has arisen in recent times. The devaluation of foreign currencies in relation to the American dollar has had a negative effect on people's ability to obtain high guarantees. As marketing and promotion costs continue to escalate on a worldwide basis, foreign distributors have become increasingly loath to give high guarantees. In many cases they would rather lose out to a competitor than get hurt by paying too much for a film that doesn't ultimately measure up to everyone's expectations. This tendency seems to be especially pronounced in the case of smaller films. Important guarantees are still achievable with films that have major elements and appear to have a chance to become big box-office winners.

In the coming months and years, the guarantees from foreign cable companies or from video cassettes are expected to eclipse the guarantees from the theatrical market. This may cause a realignment in the companies or representatives that handle the disposition of rights for foreign territories. It is a scenario that is being rewritten on a daily basis. While the source of the revenue streams may be different than it is today, in all likelihood the principles will remain the same. It will still be in the producer's best interest to sell off rights country by country, and perhaps further separate theatrical, video, cable, and free television as well. Contacts will prove important in the first instance, but follow-through may well have to come from the producer. Otherwise, he will risk seeing things handled inefficiently or sloppily. The rewards from the exploitation of films outside of the United States and Canada can be rich indeed. As a producer, you should use all the means at your disposal to line up the proper people to assist you in maximizing the potential revenues from these sources and should personally supervise all foreign sales efforts wherever possible.

14

Audits and Accounting

If you have been fortunate enough to produce a film and to register a commercial success, you will naturally look to the distribution company for your share of the net profits. Few industries are as suspect in their accounting practices as the motion picture business. A commonly held industry belief suggests that it is impossible to get a fair shake in distribution accountings from the major companies. Threats of lawsuits are common and, often, disgruntled profit participants have aired their grievances in the media.

Interestingly, few of these disputes have proceeded to litigation. Instead, the general rule has been that such profit participants have settled at some stage of the dispute. These settlements have left their claimants unhappy in the extreme. Indeed, rare is the third-party participant who has anything good to say about the accounting practices and philosophies of the company distributing his picture. The prevailing notion is that a movie had better be a huge hit if anyone is to see any contingent compensation or profits.

In the early days of films, the studios owned 100 percent of each picture they produced. They generally had the principal elements who made the pictures under contract as well. Performers, directors, and producers worked for salary alone, without regard to contingent compensation arrangements. In today's industry, however, participations are the rule and concern over getting one's just payments is at an all-time high.

Producers, of course, are also paid a fee for their services. This may range from $50,000 to as much as $500,000. A small percentage of their fee will be payable during development with the bulk of the money held back until the picture is green lighted. Interestingly, while actors, directors, and screenwriters have no ceiling on their fees, current business practice puts an upper limit on what producers get paid, regardless of their experience or involvement with current hit pictures.

It is commonplace for profit participants in a hit movie to retain the services of an accounting specialist to assist them in pressing their claims. Usually all the profit participants will act jointly and hire the same accountant to represent all of them. This course is rarely followed unless the picture seems likely to reach break even and go into profit. Otherwise, the exercise of auditing the distributor would only increase the picture's deficit position.

THE ACCOUNTANT'S POINT OF VIEW

An individual frequently retained in these circumstances is Philip Hacker, a certified public accountant, practicing in Los Angeles. He has spent the last twenty years operating in the motion picture business, most recently in his own firm specializing in auditing and accounting services for the motion picture and television industries. His is a highly specialized branch of accounting which requires an encyclopedic knowledge of the field. There is only one other firm that practices this work, also a small, specialized concern. It is very difficult for the national accounting firms to engage in this kind of work because they often represent the studios and will have a clear conflict of interest.

From Hacker's perspective, this industry has always been characterized by accounting disputes. He points out that today's deals are, if anything, more complicated than ever. This results from the explosion of new uses of films in connection with the new technologies. Not all these breakthroughs were anticipated at the time that contracts were drawn and this has produced areas of contention and dispute. In addition, studio accountants have become far more astute in interpretations of what is theatrical gross and what expenses are allowable as deductions in determining net profits.

Most significant of all, however, is Hacker's determined view that studios do not set out to intentionally misrepresent facts or defraud profit participants. He believes that the real damage to a participant's cause occurs early on at the time contracts are drawn. In his words, "Studios are becoming smarter, contracts are becoming tougher, and their interpretation is becoming much more difficult." The answer is, of course, to use all the muscle or clout you can possibly bring to bear at the time of a contract's negotiation. By the use of a skilled motion picture attorney or an agent, or both, you may be able to negotiate a solid definition of gross receipts and a fair definition of deductible expenses. That, coupled with substantial audit rights permitting you to examine all the information available over a long period of time, are your best protections against unfair treatment.

CONTRACT NEGOTIATIONS

Very often, especially in the case of first-time producers, there is effectively no real choice at the contract stage. The studio may tender a contract which is extremely one-sided in its favor and inform the producer that he must "take it or leave it." At a time like that, few producers will be able to turn their backs on picture commitments for the sake of contractual language. Later, with more experience and produced pictures behind them, those issues are far easier to resolve in a fairer, more equitable, fashion.

In Hacker's experience, a visible and vocal cross-section of actors, directors, and producers frequently complain about being "taken" by the distribution companies. According to Hacker, "They rarely know how they're being 'taken' because very few of them know the specific definition of their participation. They have a definition of profits fixed in their own minds. If you point out to them that interest is deductible, or that gross participations come off the top, and that they agreed to an overbudget penalty and a 10 percent add-on for advertising, they look blank. They were not aware of these things at the time that they signed their contracts, or they chose not to be aware of them. Then they scream how they are being 'taken' and cheated out of what is rightfully theirs."

SUBJECTIVE JUDGMENTS

It is not only the one-sidedness of contracts that causes loud protests from within the industry, but also the fact that many of the accounting practices of the studios involve highly subjective judgments. Studio attorneys and accountants are always at work interpreting contractual language. In this regard, such terms as "direct expense," "studio overhead," "cooperative advertising," or "taxes" can become very subjective.

Sometimes, new technologies will produce mass confusion in the contractual area. An example of this is the growing video cassette market. The distribution of video cassettes by the studios is generally handled through subsidiaries or affiliated companies. Most profit participants signed agreements with the studios before there were video cassettes. Thus, video cassette income will not be included in their definitions of gross receipts or net profits. How should the studio account for video cassette income? For that matter, should they have to account for it at all?

The studio has to take a position on the question as they prepare reports for the participants. The position they take is often based upon vague and imprecise contractual language and amounts to little more than subjective reasoning. Needless to say, the positions adopted by the studio are rarely in the best interest of the outside profit participant. It customarily takes an expert like Philip Hacker to apply sufficient pressure to move the studio to a more reasonable and equitable position.

Another example of how subjective analysis comes into play occurred in the distribution of *Capricorn One*. The subdistributor in Japan owed Lord Grade's company a large sum of money based on the film's performance in that country. Since they were in business on many other projects as well, there was no actual transference of funds, only a crediting of Grade's account. During that time, however, the yen was fluctuating wildly against the British pound. For this reason, the date that the payment was credited became all-important in determining how much money would change hands. A negotiator finally produced a compromise that resolved what could have been a very ugly dispute.

AUDITS

Firms like Hacker's are retained to perform one of two kinds of audits. Either they will be asked to audit the costs of production or the costs and receipts from the distribution of films. In the former case, production expenses may be very hard to track once the picture has finished shooting and editing. It is far more efficient to check these costs on a weekly basis when the picture is in production. This is especially important when working at a major studio where all labor runs come through as computer printouts. While it is a laborious task to go over each of the accounts listed with the production manager and the picture's auditor, literally hundreds of thousands of dollars can be saved in this manner.

As for the audit of the distribution of a picture, it is necessary to avail yourself of the services of someone like Philip Hacker. He would first need to read the actual contract in order to understand the definition of gross receipts employed in that particular agreement. Will cooperative advertising be deducted from gross receipts, for example? What of music, video cassettes, merchandising, publishing, and a host of other potential revenue producers? The answers to these questions can be arrived at only after an extensive review of the contractual language.

After a determination of gross receipts, the auditor would look to the distribution fees. Such fees are not actual costs incurred by the studios, but are instead amounts that the studio is contractually permitted to deduct from gross receipts. After these fees, the most difficult area still awaits the auditor's attention—the expense section. These provisions detail those expenses the studio is permitted to deduct in addition to its distribution fees. In this category fall such direct expenses as taxes, advertising, prints, freight, dues, insurance, checking, and other items of this nature. After the deduction of expenses, the auditor arrives at a net figure. He must still account for certain delayed payments known in the industry as "deferments." Interest and overhead may also be deducted, together with any penalties that may attach for overbudget situations. Finally, the studio will deduct the cost of the picture itself, and if there is anything left, it will be deemed net profits.

KEY ACCOUNTS IN AN AUDIT

When the auditor does move in on these figures, he pays particular attention to certain key accounts. Reasonable expenses, particularly in the advertising and publicity area and in the area of print costs, have proved most troublesome over the years. Surprisingly, travel and entertainment expenses never seem to amount to a major problem. The numbers are relatively small, and although they often do have some impact on the final statement, it is rarely a major one. Far more significant is the computation of interest charges, as very significant dollar amounts will hinge on these determinations.

Foreign taxes, though deductible as expenses, nonetheless pose many problems for the auditor. It is rarely clear whether such taxes were computed at the listed or proper rate, or indeed whether they were actually paid. It is very common for companies to use different devices to legally avoid paying taxes in foreign countries. Still, the participant may be charged the taxes anyway, in case such taxes may be deemed payable in the future.

ALLOCATIONS

Another problem that plagues the auditor is his analysis of studio allocations. These fall into two categories: the sale of a package of films to television or cable and the allocation of receipts between two pictures playing on the same bill. While auditors are not sales people, their experience has made them highly sensitive to situations that don't seem right. These issues will be disclosed in the audit report for discussion among the participant and his counsel. As allocations involve subjective judgment, it may be necessary for a participant's representatives to meet with the studio to negotiate some form of settlement. One way that the studios avoid discussions of this kind is to avoid selling packages of films under one contract. If individual contracts are employed for each film sold, then in theory the allocation issue will never have to be raised. Whether the film in question was actually sold on its own or with a package of other films is nearly impossible to ascertain.

LIMITED AUDIT RIGHTS

An audit touching on these issues may be available to profit participants only for a limited time. In the initial term of a picture's release, accounting statements are sent out on a quarterly basis. As time goes on, these statements will become semiannual and finally annual. After eighteen months, as an average, the studio may deem a statement to be correct. This can pose real problems when later events such as syndicated television proceeds or video cassette income may throw a marginal picture into profit. Many studios will refuse profit participants the right to examine the production costs and distribution figures from earlier years even though their pictures may now be close to profit. Although they may choose to open their books in special circumstances, generally auditing rights will lapse with the passage of time.

THE AUDITOR AND THE STUDIO

When the auditor does have to perform an audit, he generally will work with individuals in the participation accounting section of the studio. For the most part, the individuals staffing these departments are trained accounting professionals, many of whom are CPA's. In Hacker's view, most of these people do not set out to make life unpleasant for the auditor, and they accord the auditor a professional respect.

Far worse than any inconvenience in working conditions or reticence on the part of studio employees is the problem of being restricted solely to the picture being audited. The performance of comparable pictures from the same studio, or settlements with exhibitors during like times of year, or any other data not pertaining to the picture being audited is kept from the auditor. This puts an even greater value on a broad-based knowledge of industry practice at all levels of distribution.

SETTLEMENT STRATEGIES

As a general rule, after the audit report has been prepared, the parties commissioning the audit sit down with their financial and legal advisors and prepare a strategy. They can assume that any clerical errors will be corrected by the studio without a problem. All the other points in contention will have to be put to the studio for its response. Since most questions in the audit will arise over issues of subjective interpretation of the written contract, it is highly unlikely that the studio will acquiesce in all the points raised. Rather, it will propose some form of settlement. This will, in turn, be negotiated back and forth until some compromise is hammered out.

It is not unusual, however, to find that the studio digs in its heels and offers a most unreasonable sum in settlement. This will have the effect of eliciting the response from the party doing the audit, "Okay, you leave me no recourse but to sue you." Most conflicts that are brought to this point do evolve into lawsuits. There is nonetheless a strong probability that a settlement will be reached before the case comes to judgment.

Why do the preponderance of cases reach a settlement before going to judgment? This comes about because of the large sums that plaintiffs have to incur in legal expenses to press a suit today. Settlements also mean money now and not money at some indeterminate point down the road. With interest rates at today's high levels, many persons are anxious to settle for a lesser sum today to avoid the expense of litigation and the delay in receiving the money held by the studio. In addition, all litigation, no matter how clear and simple it may seem to one party, carries a very real risk. Judges or juries may believe what they choose to believe; and complexities in accounting procedures may prove too complicated to be understood by an average jury. In sum, any litigation has a decided risk in outcome. When all these factors are weighed together, it is not surprising that most suits are settled.

LITIGATION: TWO CASE STUDIES

Of the few cases that have been litigated, perhaps the most celebrated was an allocation case involving the sale of a series of films to one of the three television networks. Included in the package of films was a movie called *The Graduate*. The producer took exception to the allocation of monies received by the studio from the network claiming that his picture, the only film of the group to earn significant profits in its theatrical release, should have received a larger percentage of the television monies. Settlement talks ensued and after much acrimonious debate, a figure was agreed upon. When the settlement papers were drawn, the producer believed they did not accurately reflect the understanding reached and commenced an action. After years in court, a final judgment was eventually handed down awarding the producer an additional sum in excess of $1 million. Such persistence is rare indeed.

Still another reason why profit participants choose not to sue is made clear by a story told about a famous director who was convinced that the studio for which he had worked was withholding monies due him. After trying in vain to persuade the people with whom he dealt on a day-to-day basis, he took stock of the situation with his attorney. When he realized that the suit would be turned over to litigation counsel and that the familiar faces he was so angry at would not be around, his anger began to dissipate. He came to understand that major corporations have a battery of attorneys who deluge the plaintiff with mounds of briefs, inter-rogatories, and depositions. This kind of legal struggle can easily consume vast sums of money and a vast amount of time. In the end, it is not surprising that so many angered participants, like this director, finally shrug their shoulders and resign themselves to a settlement.

THE SHAPE OF THINGS TO COME

In Hacker's opinion, there may be some pronounced changes in this area in the near future. Companies are becoming more and more sophisticated. They are refining their accounting practices and fine-tuning their computer systems to accommodate contractual definitions. These refinements will allow great specificity in deal-making and contractual definitions. This will, it is hoped, put more and more questions into the realm of objective facts rather than subjective interpretations.

Finally, the movie business of today seems to have thrown open its doors to outside financial groups seeking to partially finance a portion of a studio's slate of pictures. As Hacker puts it, "These people are generally more financially astute than the producers and the directors who traditionally share in the participations. They are negotiating much tougher deals because they're coming up with money. The old adage holds. If you have the money, you're going to have much more strength at the bargaining table than you will if you have only marched in with a creative idea."

Perhaps, as Philip Hacker suggests, the proper place to bear down is at the contract stage of negotiations, not after the returns are all in. Perhaps, too, the old accounting adage that describes accounting as an art and not a science has never been more applicable than it is in the area of participants' profit statements. Whatever changes the future holds, it is hoped that they will serve to restore some confidence in the accounting systems employed by the studios and contribute to a healthier climate in which to make pictures.

Epilogue

The producer who has need of a chapter on audits and accounting will have traveled a long way from the time he first obtained motion picture rights to some form of property. Chances are his ability to persist in the face of rejections or frustrations will have been severely tested. His network of contacts and business relationships will probably have expanded far beyond his expectations. He will have experienced first hand the reasons why it is said that the making of any movie is a battle but getting a movie made is a war.

Whether the movie succeeds or not, the process of having produced a film will almost certainly be viewed as a broadening and beneficial one. It will have developed new skills—creative and financial—and tapped into resources and qualities that may not have been previously utilized. Producing motion pictures is a profession of unlimited challenge and opportunity. It requires a belief in your project, but first and foremost, a belief in yourself.

Index